INVENTIVE GENIUS

Inventive

THE HISTORY

OF THE MUSEUM

OF SCIENCE

AND INDUSTRY

CHICAGO

Genius

JAY PRIDMORE

MUSEUM OF SCIENCE AND INDUSTRY, CHICAGO

First Edition

Library of Congress Cataloging-in-Publication Data

Pridmore, Jay, 1952–
     Inventive genius : the history of the Museum of Science and Industry,
   Chicago / Jay Pridmore. — 1st ed.
        p. cm.
     Includes index.
     ISBN 0-9638657-4-9 (hardcover). — ISBN 0-9638657-5-7 (pbk.)
     1. Museum of Science and Industry (Chicago, Ill.)—History.
  I. Title.
  T180.C45M87   1996   96–13546
  607.4'773'11—dc20   CIP

Manufactured in the United States of America

Museum of Science and Industry
57th Street and Lake Shore Drive
Chicago, IL 60637

"American inventive genius needs greater stimulation and room for development. . . . I would like every young growing mind in Chicago to be able to see working models, visualizing developments in machines and processes which have been built by the greatest industrial nation in the world."

JULIUS ROSENWALD
Founder of the Museum of
Science and Industry

As quoted in the *Chicago Tribune*, April 1926

Before it became the Museum of Science and Industry, the great pavilion on the lagoon was the Palace of Fine Arts, built for the 1893 World's Columbian Exposition. Augustus Saint-Gaudens, America's greatest classical artist at the time, called it "unequaled since the Parthenon."

CONTENTS

The Museum building was inspired by many different monuments of the classical world, such as the 14-foot "telamones" above the porticos, modeled after originals in Agrigento. While critics in 1893 were ready to pounce on architect Charles B. Atwood for any error in proportion, they found none. "Confound him, he is right every time," said one.

Panels from the Parthenon metopes were reproduced in the Palace of Fine Arts in 1893. So noble was its design, originally constructed in plaster, that Chicago resolved that this, of all buildings of the world's fair, should be made permanent, which it was when the Museum of Science and Industry opened in 1933.

LIKE THOUSANDS OF OTHERS in Chicago and around the world, I have been touched by the Museum of Science and Industry at various times and in many contexts. I first visited the Museum as a 16-year-old high school graduate. That was in 1948. Later, I became reacquainted with it while attending graduate school at the University of Chicago and living in Hyde Park in 1955 and 1956. In the mid-1960s, I returned to Chicago on vacation with my family and introduced them to this fascinating institution. We were intrigued by its one-of-a-kind artifacts: the specimens in the prenatal development exhibit, the cross sections of human bodies, a captured German U-boat and a coal mine that seemed to operate deep beneath the Museum floor.

In 1986, when I was invited to be a candidate for the position I now hold, I attempted unsuccessfully to find a history of the Museum that already had been a part of my life for nearly four decades. By 1988, I had served as the Museum's chief executive officer for more than a year and confirmed what I had suspected—there was no crisp, accurate, informative history of the largest science museum in the United States.

On countless occasions, I was asked about the institution's past: Who were the previous directors? What was the role of Julius Rosenwald and Sears, Roebuck and Company? What was the relationship between the Deutsches Museum in Munich and the Museum of Science and Industry in Chicago? Who was Lenox Lohr? What was his relationship with Walt Disney? These were important questions with interesting and colorful answers.

During this time, I was fortunate to meet and become friends with Jay Pridmore, a Chicago journalist whose perceptive articles on Chicago's cultural institutions appeared regularly in the *Chicago Tribune*. Jay and I often talked about the reverence and attachment that the Museum had invoked in visitors from its earliest days. We also shared our regret about the lack of a documented Museum history. The outcome of this dialogue was a fortunate one: Jay accepted a commission from the Museum to write its history.

It was agreed that the story would properly begin in 1893 at the World's Columbian Exposition, as the world was preparing for the 20th century with innovations in industry, science and technology. It would continue until MSI 2000, the program currently preparing the Museum to be a unique center for new generations to develop science literacy for the 21st century.

In the century between the World's Columbian Exposition and MSI 2000, the importance of science education grew exponentially. I know of no seminal documentation analyzing science education in 1893 or in the early 1930s when the Museum opened its doors for the first time. In fact, science education was certainly an element of preparatory school and college in the 1930s and 1940s, but it did not begin to command public attention until the technology of World War II became a part of everyday conversation. Its significance grew with the development of the atomic bomb and its impact on the subsequent military policies of the '40s, '50s and '60s.

Today, we cannot proceed further than the front pages of our daily newspapers before we are inundated with technical jargon. It is generally accepted that a competitive edge in technology is critical to economic viability. Fluency in science and technology is vital in a learned and economically strong nation. Scientific literacy is absolutely essential for success in the global marketplace.

The Museum of Science and Industry has changed from a series of halls with large and interesting artifacts to a vibrant science-technology-industry education center filling a unique niche in science learning through its novel focus on today's science and industry and tomorrow's technology and innovation. It has been and remains the model for the origin and philosophy of many of the world's pre-eminent science museums. It has educated and influenced millions of people around the globe by utilizing unique interactive learning methods in thoroughly uncommon classrooms.

This is the history of one of the world's most beloved, respected, scrutinized and visited institutions. It is the product of the visionary imagination of Julius Rosenwald, the showmanship and creativity of Lenox Lohr, the education and exhibit innovations of Dan MacMaster and Victor Danilov and the dream of MSI 2000 today.

James S. Kahn
President and Chief Executive Officer
Museum of Science and Industry

The Museum's caryatids were modeled after those of the Erechtheum of Athens, one of the many Greek and Roman buildings used by architect Charles B. Atwood in designing what is considered one of the high points of the Beaux Arts era.

The first thing that most visitors see when they enter the Museum of Science and Industry are the great bronze doors. The reliefs were sculpted in the 1930s to represent the many branches of science explored and explained within.

GREAT MUSEUMS AND GREAT libraries epitomize great civilizations. So vital are they to a society's well-being that if the museums and libraries decline, the society they support is often doomed to decline as well.

That is exactly what happened in the Middle Ages in Europe. An earlier and even clearer example of the link between a society and its centers of knowledge and learning was Alexandria, the great city at the mouth of the Nile River. Alexander the Great founded Alexandria in 331 B.C. For more than 400 years—twice as long as the United States has existed—Alexandria served as the trading and intellectual capital of the Mediterranean. Scholars agree that Alexandria's rise and dominance stemmed in large part from the great library and museum founded shortly after the city was built.

At its height, the library held more than 750,000 volumes. The museum collected specimens and knowledge in all the contemporary sciences. Like great museums throughout history, the Alexandria museum taught as well as collected. The greatest teachers of the time gathered there to write, study and lecture in mathematics, geometry, astronomy, philosophy, engineering, medicine, astrology, theology and geography.

Unfortunately for the world of that time—and for our world today—the Romans destroyed this great library and museum. So complete was the physical ruin that today we can find only the cellar of a library annex and a few shelves. So complete was the intellectual ruin that today no one knows for certain even what Alexandria looked like. In the wake of that destruction, the city of Alexandria became just another Mediterranean port, no longer the intellectual light of the known world.

WHY IS THIS LINK between great museums and great societies such a recurring historical theme? For one illustration of the pivotal function that museums perform for society, we need look no further than the Paris Museum of Arts and Crafts in the 18th century and its key contribution to the development of the computer. No one at the museum, or indeed anywhere in France, knew the Paris Museum was making this contribution. Everyone thought the subject was weaving.

Silk weaving in the 1700s was an expensive, tedious endeavor fraught with miscues and rejects. Inspired in part by an organ maker, several French engineers devised a better way. They punched rows of holes in a cylinder, then wrapped the cylinder with paper containing holes corresponding to the pattern to be woven. Their system ensured that only the proper threads would be pulled at the proper time to create the desired pattern.

Unfortunately, not everyone saw this as an advance. Silk weavers considered it a threat to their jobs and rioted. Development of the automated loom ceased. The prototype loom was disassembled, and the pieces went to the Paris Museum, which preserved the loom in relative obscurity for more than 50 years.

Unlike its predecessor in Alexandria, the Paris Museum survived political turmoil—in this case, the revolutionary chaos that rocked France in the late 1700s. And in 1800, the museum asked a French silk weaver named Jacquard to reassemble the unusual old loom. As he reassembled it, he thought the loom might work even better if he replaced the punched paper with punched cards. That way, a weaver who wanted to extend the pattern needed only to add more cards in an endless chain. Today, we call this device the Jacquard loom.

Of course, others outside the textile industry took notice of the technique of using punched cards to control intricate machine processes. By 1890, the United States was using machines of this type to speed census taking. Today, the same binary code first employed with punched paper and punch cards is the language of the computers which increasingly dominate our complex world.

THIS ROLE OF THE MUSEUM—as preservationist, teacher and catalyst for innovation—was well appreciated by the first director of the Museum of Science and Industry, Waldemar Kaempffert. As discussed in Chapter 1, Kaempffert knew that progress is evolutionary, that one scientific discovery leads to the next and that scientific exposition invariably is followed by industrial disposition.

In other words, industry employs what science develops. In doing this, industry creates jobs, prosperity and the capital that science requires for education and the tools needed for the next step. The mutually supportive cycle of science and industry is clear.

This is true not only in the halls of the Museum of Science and Industry. Increasingly, the great scientific laboratories of the world involve industry in their research plans and projects. And increasingly, great industries look to scientific laboratories as today's incubators for tomorrow's advances.

My laboratory, Argonne National Laboratory, recognized this synergy early in its life. Although the Museum of Science and Industry was a robust teenager when Argonne was born in 1946, the young national laboratory was just two years old when it sponsored its first exhibit at the Museum. My predecessors at Argonne were sufficiently aware of the lessons of history that they used their first exhibit to teach as well as to inform. We have been back many times since, and I have no doubt that the close relationship between the Museum of Science and Industry and Argonne National Laboratory, as well as Argonne's parent, the University of Chicago, will continue well into the next century.

THE 21ST CENTURY will be a time when such relationships and such institutions will be increasingly important to the United States. Clearly it will be a time when societies and nations must remain technologically sophisticated in order to lead and prosper. Just as clearly, but unfortunately, the United States is approaching the new century with a population that often borders on technological illiteracy.

Starting in the late 1970s, the Museum of Science and Industry recognized the urgent need to improve the public's scientific awareness, and it adopted the public's scientific education as a key Museum goal. Those efforts grow ever more important.

In a democratic society, the people have the responsibility to evaluate new technologies and to chart the best and wisest course. Yet today in America's daily discourse, the public's shallow technological base too often results in the dumbing down of complex issues into two-dimensional melodramas. The news media feed on this and further it, precisely because that is what the public seems to want. Like fast food, fast *facts* permit the public to grab a quick impression, to make a fast and often shallow decision and then to get back to the concerns of daily life.

Public programs such as those of the Museum of Science and Industry help to break that unfortunate cycle by bringing science to life in accurate yet jargon-free terms the public can understand. Although we certainly cannot condense complex ideas into bumper-sticker slogans, we can and must present science and industry in clear, simple and understandable language. That is a need a young Museum curator named Lucy Nielsen, whose story is told in this book, understood long before many of her more senior colleagues.

This valuable book is a readable and informative history of one remarkable museum's evolution from idea to reality to prominence. Yet it is much more. The book also illustrates how great institutions come into being and how disparate individuals with vision and dedication mold their raw material into greatness. That was just as true of Eratosthenes in Alexandria as it was of Rosenwald and Lohr some 2,400 years later in Chicago.

Finally, this book says much about Chicago's role as a world center of science and industry. That, too, is a product of the noble quality Jay Pridmore has aptly dubbed *Inventive Genius*.

Alan Schriesheim
Director and Chief Executive Officer
Argonne National Laboratory

The *Piccard Gondola* was the centerpiece of the "greatest human drama ever" when Dr. Jean Piccard and his team tried to break the world altitude record by hydrogen-filled balloon at the 1933 exposition, A Century of Progress. The attempt failed, but Piccard later set the mark at 61,237 feet before the craft was retired to the Museum of Science and Industry in 1935.

ONE

The Museum Takes Flight

An event billed as the "greatest human drama ever" finally began after midnight on August 5, 1933. The stands of Chicago's Soldier Field had been filled for hours with 50,000 people, and hundreds more were milling around the stadium gridiron. All were waiting for the launch of Lieutenant Commander T. G. W. Settle into the stratosphere. Settle, a Navy pilot, would fly alone in a small enclosed gondola suspended from a huge hydrogen balloon. His plan was to set the undisputed world altitude record, floating to 54,000 feet—about 10 miles—over Chicago.

It was certainly the most exciting event of A Century of Progress, Chicago's great world's fair, "the culmination of invention and science . . . and acme of modern progress," as it was hailed by its organizers. The fair featured striking modern architecture, the famous Sky Ride above the lagoon and the fan dance of Sally Rand. Commander Settle's ascent was a dramatic climax. Only hours before, organizers had declared weather conditions right for the attempt. Most of the Soldier Field crowd knew little of meteorology. Nor were they informed about the scientific objectives of the flight. The public sensed mostly that the event was momentous, and they turned out en masse despite the absurdly late hour.

Around 10 o'clock that night, technicians began inflating the balloon, which was made from an acre of rubberized fabric. It was connected by a tangled web of tubing to 700 tanks of "laboratory perfect" hydrogen. As the gas hissed, people said that it sounded like a distant train. The balloon rose up, partially inflated, and one of the hundreds of journalists present likened it to an uncoiling boa constrictor.

The metal gondola was then rolled underneath the balloon and hooked to the cables. Settle's life would depend upon the strength of this sphere, made of a special alloy steel. A mere seven feet in diameter, it was also a fully equipped scientific laboratory where the commander planned to spend a full 24 hours. There was something surreal about the spectacle, illuminated with all the intensity of six spotlights of 8 million candlepower each. The largest balloon ever made was floating in the air. A bright full moon shone above the stadium's Grecian columns. Time passed swiftly for everyone who was present that night.

At 2:15 a.m. one of the fair officials spoke on the public address system and asked the crowd for complete silence. The pilot wanted to test the gas valve at the top of the balloon—one of his few navigational controls—and he could do this only by sound. There had been problems with the valve in the past; even now Settle sensed that it was releasing more gas than he would have liked. But 50,000 people were waiting in Soldier Field and millions were listening to the event via an unprecedented radio hookup. Settle reckoned that he could nurse the mechanism through his flight.

Sometime before 3 a.m. the aviator got on top of the gondola. Flags on the shrouds—an American one and a Navy Jack—fluttered, and when the Army band struck up "The Star-Spangled Banner," the crowd rose to their feet. All were sure it was the beginning of a great flight. At 3:05 a.m. Settle lifted off.

Many technological feats were to be accomplished that night. The gondola was fully equipped for high altitude with liquid oxygen and special substances to absorb carbon dioxide and moisture emitted by the body. The gondola also had instruments to measure cosmic rays. It was hoped that experiments in flight would resolve an amicable dispute between two Nobel Prize winners, Robert A. Millikan of the California Institute of Technology and Arthur Compton of the University of Chicago, over the electrical properties of radioactive streams in the stratosphere. Also packed on the gondola was a spectrographic camera that would take pictures of the spectrum of the sun's rays.

These and other scientific aspects of the flight were the work of renowned physicist Jean Piccard, himself one of the era's most famous balloonists. Piccard had agreed to the Chicago ascent because he believed the publicity of A Century of Progress would do much to advance his stratospheric study. He chose Settle, a professional pilot, to improve chances for an altitude record. Piccard was right about the publicity; anticipation of the event riveted Chicago's attention for months. Piccard himself became an object of public curiosity, particularly because his twin brother Auguste Piccard was an equally eminent scientist known for his descents into the ocean in bathyspheres.

ANOTHER FEAT OF TECHNOLOGY that night would also touch the general public. It was a live broadcast of the event by the National Broadcasting Company. To augment conventional news coverage, the gondola was equipped with a transmitter, and early in his flight Settle's voice would be transmitted to a studio in Chicago, and then around the world. It constituted an amazing bit of broadcast engineering, and included a portable transmitting unit that could be carried by a radio reporter in the chase car to interview Settle the instant he returned to earth.

Ace announcers Charley Lyon and Hal Totten were in the broadcast booth in Soldier Field that night, and as the moment of liftoff drew close, a combination of tension and joy heightened their voices. Lyon described the final moments in detail. Commander Settle kissed his wife, grinned at his handlers and sat atop the gondola. As the balloon was released and floated skyward, Settle slipped inside.

Then the unthinkable happened. The balloon was only a few thousand feet high, still within range of the spotlights. On the radio, Lyon's voice stopped for a moment, then he shouted into his microphone: "It's coming down!" Then he paused again.

"No! Yes it is. Oh it can't be! But it certainly looks that way. It must be an optical illusion, ladies and gentlemen, that gives us the impression Commander Settle's balloon is losing altitude. . . . No, no, it is coming. Hal, Hal Totten, look. Look at that balloon. It is coming down, isn't it?"

It was. Gas in the form of steam was pouring visibly from the faulty valve. Then the balloon wafted high above the stadium's west stands. Pandemonium broke loose among the crowd. Many rushed out of Soldier Field in hope of seeing Settle's landing, wherever it might be, and however tragic.

Among those who ran from Soldier Field was NBC's Charley Lyon, carrying the portable transmitter over his shoulder. That left Totten in the broadcast booth, and he was instantly hooked up with another announcer, Bob Brown, at NBC's studios in the Merchandise Mart in Chicago. On live radio, they tried to call up Lyon, but could not. So Brown and Totten ad-libbed. With virtually no news to announce, Brown talked of his own experience covering a balloon race three years before. The two also requested anyone who knew where Settle's ship had come down to call the station immediately by telephone.

Within minutes, word did come that Settle had landed in the rail yard at 14th and Canal Streets, a little over a mile from the stadium. Miraculously, it seemed, he was uninjured. Totten shouted the news to the people pressing around his booth. Hearing this, a woman collapsed to the ground and laughed hysterically. "He's all right," she cried.

Finally, Charley Lyon came on the air from his over-the-shoulder transmitter. Stepping over railroad tracks amid thousands of people trying to get a glimpse of the balloon, of the gondola and of Settle, the mobile announcer could report that the pilot was calm and collected. He had landed his craft with such skill that the damage was negligible. There was some difficulty with souvenir hunters who began cutting the balloon into small scraps, but military police were able to control the situation. As dawn was breaking, Settle was being interviewed by a pack of reporters. The pilot said he was sorry to have disappointed so many people who had come out to witness the flight. Only later did he realize that the drama of the evening had disappointed no one.

Within hours, the raw drama of Lieutenant Commander Settle's ascent was front-page news around this world. It would take longer, of course, to sort out the significance of this night in the history of science and aeronautics. Nevertheless, the curators of a brand new museum a few miles south of Soldier Field were already convinced that the implications of the ascent, despite its ostensible failure, were profound.

The new museum was the Museum of Science and Industry, which had opened just over a month earlier in the renovated Palace of Fine Arts, the last remaining structure of a previous world's fair, the World's Columbian Exposition of 1893. Even before Settle and Piccard arrived in Chicago, the Museum's curator of physics, Andrew M. MacMahon, had written a memo to several trustees explaining that every effort should be made to acquire the gondola and display it as a milestone of science. The Museum, MacMahon stated, was uniquely qualified to provide the public with an understanding of what stratospheric research meant.

CERTAINLY THE HIGH DRAMA of the Piccard gondola was what philanthropist Julius Rosenwald had in mind when he founded the Museum of Science and Industry with an initial contribution of $3 million. Rosenwald, the immensely wealthy president of Sears, Roebuck and Company, wanted for Chicago a museum to equal and perhaps even surpass the great technology museums of Europe. His money and power, not to say his determination, got all of Chicago behind the project when he announced it in 1926. He also arranged to locate the Industrial Museum, as it was called before it was properly christened, in the old Palace of Fine Arts of the World's Columbian Exposition of 1893.

The sprawling Palace, when renovated, became one of Chicago's true monuments. Its architecture would be matched only by Rosenwald's high social purpose. Inside, the founder envisioned exhibits on all branches of science and technology, which were "a rightful part of the heritage of any growing generation and could be of very great value in the United States, particularly in Chicago, for the instruction of students and citizens," he told the *Chicago Daily News*.

Thus, it was natural to do everything necessary to acquire the Piccard gondola. To advance this cause, the Museum's board president Sewell Avery contacted Colonel Frank Knox, publisher of the *Chicago Daily News*, which had cosponsored the balloon launch. Avery, who was also president of Montgomery Ward, suggested that the gondola would make an excellent exhibit for the new

The *Piccard Gondola* was retired in 1935 after a number of record-setting flights—one of which included Jean Piccard's wife Jeannette, who held the altitude mark for a female for 50 years. The Piccards promised their gondola to the Museum, but only after a sponsored tour around the country so the public could see their famous stratospheric aircraft.

museum and for Chicago as a whole. Knox responded enthusiastically and agreed to exert whatever influence he could to make sure that the scientific treasure remained in Chicago.

Meanwhile, the Museum's director, Otto Kreusser, contacted Piccard directly, and the day after the ascent he found the scientist at wit's end. The failed flight had created a tangle of difficult issues for Piccard and his sponsors, which included Goodyear Tire and Rubber, manufacturer of the rubberized balloon fabric; Dow Chemical, which had made the metal alloy for the gondola; and Union Carbide, which had provided the gas. Who was responsible for the balloon? For the repairs?

Amid the confusion, Kreusser was quick to offer whatever services the Museum might provide to get the balloon to a place safe from mildew and souvenir hunters. Piccard accepted, and before another day had passed a team of 20 Museum workers was sent to help move the balloon from a rail-road shed to the city's Naval Armory, where it could be spread out to dry. Piccard deeply appreciated Kreusser's favor, and he agreed to visit the Museum and discuss what might become of the gondola when its flying days were over.

When Piccard arrived at the new Museum, the interior was largely unfin-ished, but the few galleries that were open were lined with an array of fasci-nating exhibits—artifacts, models and other devices for teaching the history of technology. As the Museum was being planned, its organizers contacted scientists, engineers and industrialists from around the world, telling them that if their stories could be told anywhere, it was here. Nearly three years before the Museum opened, advertisements soliciting objects for exhibits had gone into magazines such as *Nature*, the *British Journal of Photography* and a dozen other professional publications.

The solicitations were highly successful. Donations ranged from unique objects of great significance to material of less obvious merit. Among the first artifacts to come in was a shipment of historic radio apparatus, given by a col-lector in New York who for decades had haunted auctions and secondhand shops. These artifacts would enable the Museum to tell the story of wireless communication more vividly than it was told anywhere else in the world. Next came a collection of 11 X-ray tubes from Howard University in Washington, D.C., where early experiments in the developing technology had been con-ducted. An anthropologist from New York's American Museum of Natural History traveled to Peruvian villages to bring back primitive weaving machines for the Chicago museum as well as his own. Marshall Field's donated a set of rollers that had been used to print fabric.

Some artifacts were much larger, in size and in message. The oldest loco-motive of the South came from the Illinois Central Railroad—it was the Mississippi, built in 1834, which along with several other railroad engines began to suggest a grand interior. Not long before its opening in 1933, the Museum also found the head frame and other equipment from an abandoned coal mine, which settled any question of the Museum's scale.

To tell the stories behind the artifacts, the founders hired a team of cura-tors, mostly from the ranks of academia. With such experts on board, the Museum was organized into six divisions that the founders believed embraced the full range of the technological world: from the fundamental sciences such as physics and chemistry to the miracles of communication and civil engineering. Slowly but deliberately, curators pieced together their ideas for illustrating and explaining these subjects to the public.

Putting ideas into action was the work of the first director of the Museum of Science and Industry, Waldemar Kaempffert, who came to Chicago from New York, where he had been science editor of the *New York Times*. Kaempffert saw the age-old interaction of science and industry as one of the most dramatic stories ever. But too often, he said, its milestone events went unnoticed by the general public. For Kaempffert, the Chicago museum was the opportunity of a lifetime—to dramatize on a large stage the impact of technological progress on society as a whole.

AMONG THE MANY BRANCHES of technology beckoning the Museum, aviation was certainly one of the most exciting. Early in his tenure as director, Kaempffert made strong overtures to Orville Wright to get him to contribute the first airplane, the *Kitty Hawk*, as the centerpiece of the Museum's transportation exhibit. Wright, Kaempffert learned, was irate about the Smithsonian Institution's claims that Samuel Langley had gone aloft in a self-propelled flying machine some nine days before the Wright brothers had in 1903. Thus, the Wright plane was pulled out of the Washington museum and placed in the Science Museum of London. Kaempffert hoped that Wright might bring it to Chicago, especially if he subscribed to Wright's version of aviation history.

The Museum held out hope for the *Kitty Hawk* for ten years, during which time the Ford Museum of Dearborn, Michigan, also got in the bidding. In the end both were disappointed. The Smithsonian ultimately rewrote its history to credit the Wright brothers properly, and Orville finally agreed to put the first flying machine in Washington. Still, the Museum of Science and Industry remained convinced that they could, and must, tell the amazing story of flight.

Other wonderful airplanes came in. Among them was a monoplane called *Texaco No. 13*, a streamlined, single-engine "speed plane" built in 1930 by the Travel Air Manufacturing Company of Wichita, Kansas. Operated by the Texas Company—Texaco—*Texaco No. 13* had a story as romantic as the golden age of aviation itself. It was piloted by one of the most glamorous characters of his time, Captain Frank Monroe Hawks, whose start with the Texaco bird was a near-tragic failure. Hawks got tangled in wires on his test flight and came down on the plane's nose. But the damage was slight, and after repairs Hawks set airspeed records the world over. It got so that takeoffs and landings by *Texaco No. 13* were front-page news wherever he went. On August 6, 1930, for instance, Hawks flew across the continent from New York to Los Angeles in just 14 hours, 30 minutes, 43 seconds, an amazing mark. Then he set a series of other intercity records, coaxing the plane to sustained speeds of well over 200 miles per hour.

Texaco No. 13, also called the Mystery Ship for its dazzling records, was retired in 1932, but it did not fade away. Its past was proudly recalled as an exhibit at A Century of Progress. The exhibit amplified the reputation of Hawks, who predicted, "Someday we will have airplanes of far greater speed. The schedules will cover greater distances and the resultant effect upon the aviation fraternity will be to cement closer and closer their friendship and understanding."

It was the kind of glow that Texaco or any other company relished, and the

Captain Frank Monroe Hawks with his famous aircraft the *Texaco No. 13*.
In the early 1930s Hawks set cross-country records in his "speed plane"
before it was placed on public display, first at A Century of Progress
and later at the Museum of Science and Industry. Reprinted with
permission from Texaco Inc.

company quickly found the Museum of Science and Industry a convenient place
to perpetuate it. When the fair ended in 1934, the company's local sales
manager wrote to find out "the name of the person whom we should contact
regarding the donation and acceptance of this ship."

Other planes also came to the Museum from the fair. A Curtiss Pusher,
actually a replica of a famous 1910 biplane, was brought to Chicago by the
Curtiss-Wright Corporation. Also coming via the fair was the Boeing Mail Plane,
donated by United Airlines, which flew this plane and others like it for transcon-
tinental mail service in the late '20s.

Of course there was the Piccard gondola, representing the precise blend of
research and romance that brought the Museum of Science and Industry to life.

Although the age of "heroic inventors" such as the Wrights and Edison was giving way to the age of mammoth corporations with highly organized research arms, Piccard saw clearly what the organizers of the Museum of Science and Industry were attempting. That was to show the human side of science and inspire young people toward technological careers. Thus Piccard agreed after his first visit that the gondola should make the Museum its home.

Actually, the Piccard gondola would not become a permanent fixture right away. Later in 1933, Piccard and Settle took the balloon and gondola to Akron, Ohio, and made another attempt to break the altitude record at the Goodyear-Zeppelin dock. Settle did set a new mark at 61,237 feet.

Then, the following year, Piccard and his wife Jeannette announced that for their next ascent, they would pilot the balloon themselves. The couple stressed that their objective was no longer altitude records but real science. Nevertheless, sponsors such as the National Geographic Society, Goodyear and Dow said the flight was too dangerous for a woman with three sons at home, and they withdrew. The Piccards went ahead just the same, and although their flight was a scientific success, it is remembered mostly for setting a world altitude record by a woman, a mark that held for 50 years. The gondola came to a permanent landing in 1935 and was retired to the Museum that year.

AVIATION WAS NO PASSING FANCY at the Museum of Science and Industry. Full-size aircraft, as they filled the great spaces of the old building, advanced the Museum's cause in many ways. For one thing, flying machines suggested heroism that most people did not associate with scientific pioneers.

On a more basic level, perhaps, aircraft in the Museum were oversized, impressive and awe-inspiring. They created instant curiosity in children and adults alike. Curiosity led to questions, and questions to real learning. This was precisely what the founders of the Museum had in mind from the time it was first conceived.

Airplanes, in other words, were powerful teaching tools. Teaching was very much on the mind of Museum president James S. Kahn many years later, when he accepted the gift of a full-size 727 for a new transportation hall. If a Curtiss Pusher aloft in the rafters massaged the imagination, a 133-foot jetliner might do much more.

Indeed, the United 727 was a great opportunity for showmanship. In September, 1992, the plane made its final landing at Meigs Field on Chicago's lakefront amid much fanfare at a strip unaccustomed to large planes. A year later it was barged to the Museum and drew enormous attention as it was rolled over a platform across the beach and Lake Shore Drive. The new exhibit, *Take Flight*, opened October 28, 1994. The fuselage was hung along a balcony with a single wing stretched over the entire transportation exhibit.

Inside, it was more than just an airplane. It was equipped with electron-

9

ics and other interactive devices explaining navigation, radar and Bernoulli's principle of lift. The exhibits were strange and compelling, and the lessons were unforgettable.

Take Flight was a great success, with late-model computers and advanced educational techniques. More important, perhaps, it demonstrated something that the earliest curators of the Museum understood and why flying machines have always worked so well here. It showed that a museum of technology touches more than the logical and well-ordered areas of the brain. It can move the romantic spirit as well. The history of the Museum of Science and Industry is about ambitious efforts to touch a visitors' imagination as well as their reason.

Julius Rosenwald's Golden Touch

As soon as Julius Rosenwald proposed a new industrial museum for Chicago—called "the crystallization of the dream of the capitalist" by the *Chicago Tribune*—its success seemed assured. The plan was outlined at a meeting of the Commercial Club of Chicago on August 17, 1926. Rosenwald pledged $3 million to establish an institution modeled after the industrial museums of Europe, but one that he hoped would overshadow them. It would feature the "marvels of mechanics and science reduced in size for easy comprehension." It would stimulate "American inventive genius." The Commercial Club applauded the concept. Newspapers lionized Rosenwald as a philanthropist to rival the Rockefellers.

Rosenwald's bequest was combined with a magnificent site, the stately but crumbling Palace of Fine Arts, Chicago's last vestige of the World's Columbian Exposition of 1893. The building won lavish praise when it was built. "Unequaled since the Parthenon," cried Augustus Saint-Gaudens, America's great classical sculptor at the time. Despite past exaggerations and its current disrepair, the building remained high in Chicago's esteem. More out of respect than reason, the park commissioners had for some years deferred what seemed like its inevitable demolition. Now, Julius Rosenwald provided the perfect solution. Politicians and businessmen alike fell in love with his plan for a museum. Huzzahs were sounded by editors, architects and people in many other quarters of society.

A museum like the one proposed by Rosenwald had been discussed for years. While many European cities had excellent museums of scientific and industrial discovery, Americans were concerned and even embarrassed that nothing of the type existed in this country. By the mid-1920s, several initiatives

The idea and the money for the Museum of Science and Industry came from Julius Rosenwald, president of Sears, Roebuck and Company. One of America's greatest philanthropists, Rosenwald pledged $3 million for the institution as a place to inspire America's "inventive genius."

were undertaken to correct the situation. The most ambitious was for a National Museum of Engineering and Industry, envisioned as part of the Smithsonian Institution. This plan had considerable support, headed by Chicago utilities magnate Samuel Insull and with luminaries such as Thomas Edison and Orville

Wright listed as supporters of the project. The National Museum's prospectus lamented that "the world's leading industrial nation, first alike in inventive genius and in the magnitude of its industrial operations, possesses no adequate museum of industry." This museum would raise a substantial building on the Mall in Washington, D.C., and then form a network of appropriate branch museums in other cities. New York's would focus on electrical engineering, perhaps, Pittsburgh's on the steel industry and Chicago's on agricultural machinery.

While the backers of the Smithsonian plan attempted to raise money and gain steam, other museums along the same lines were contemplated elsewhere. In New York, a Museum of the Peaceful Arts was outlined in the will of the late Henry R. Towne of Yale and Towne Corporation, the manufacturer of locks. Towne's bequest provided for a museum to celebrate the fact "that the United States is the greatest industrial nation in the world; that its inventors and industrial leaders have won the foremost place in almost every field of applied science, that its organized industries excel those of all other countries in magnitude and efficiency." The New York organizers looked to the museums of Europe as their model, and they would also conduct foreign exchanges with professors of engineering. Technology, the organizers believed, could be an agent of international goodwill. They had $3 million available for a museum to examine metallurgy, aeronautics, engineering and many other "fruits of industry."

The Smithsonian and the Towne projects stalled for predictable reasons— most related to money. Although the United States already boasted many great museums, most of them had been founded in a different time. The Metropolitan Museum of Art in New York City, for example, had been chartered in 1870 at a cost of $500,000. Chicago's Field Museum had been established in 1893 for $1 million. Now the National Museum of Engineering and Industry was attempting, without success, to raise $10 million, and the New York Museum of the Peaceful Arts was having trouble finding a suitable site in Manhattan.

Chicago, on the other hand, had $3 million and a site of more than average merit. It had the added incentive to succeed in an enterprise that was flagging elsewhere. Chicago's "second city syndrome" had been festering for a long time, and the reasons were not hard to discern. Easterners still regarded Chicago as a mongrel city—a Babel of immigrants— despite its national importance as a commerce center. The World's Columbian Exposition had been a vindication, but Chicago congressmen had needed to maneuver and argue endlessly to get it. "As all roads go to Rome, all railroads go to Chicago!" one loyal booster had shouted at the time. Thus, Chicago became the Windy City, so-called not for the wind off the lake but rather for its overblown rhetoric. The moniker stuck, and Chicago never lost its pride.

Nor did it lose its small-town ability to assemble power brokers quickly. Once Chicagoans decided to advance the idea of an industrial museum, the effort was fast and credible. Money, power and enthusiasm coalesced behind the cause so quickly that the *New York Times* soon wrote a laudatory editorial on the subject headlined "Chicago Doing It First." This, of all things, was like a ringing endorsement from Oz. Success seemed assured.

CREDIT FOR THE NEW MUSEUM belonged, of course, to Julius Rosenwald, whose power owed not merely to his fortune, which amounted to $150 million at the time, but to his vision and persuasiveness as well. Through a vast network of charitable organizations, combined with near-transcendent personal modesty, Rosenwald became one of America's leading philanthropists in an era dominated by private wealth.

By 1927, Rosenwald was a living legend, partly for his well-timed move to become the partner of Richard Sears when the latter was a small mail-order distributor. Also well known were stories about Rosenwald demonstrating that even as a struggling garment manufacturer, he was moved almost helplessly to give his money away. In 1890, for example, young Rosenwald was walking home from work with one of his financial backers. He said that his personal needs amounted to only $15,000 a year: $5,000 to support his family, $5,000 to save and $5,000 to donate to charity. There is no record of his backer's response. But by 1906, when Sears, Roebuck and Company was bringing in something like $1 million a week, Rosenwald spent most of his time, if not his money, on worthy causes that needed his support.

He had no trouble finding such causes. American cities, and especially Chicago, were growing exponentially at the time, and the flip side of urban growth was poverty. European immigrants were coming to America by the millions. African Americans were migrating north in a steady stream. All searched for jobs promising higher wages and better lives. Not everyone succeeded. Thus came the need for people like Jane Addams, whose settlement-house movement gained national prominence with Hull House in Chicago. As the field of social work evolved, Rosenwald gave money to dozens of such organizations. And although his gifts were munificent, they were not indiscriminate. A businessman to the end, Rosenwald always judged charities for their long-term objectives and efficiency. He often said he preferred "wholesale" programs to individual handouts, because they were more effective dollar for dollar.

Rosenwald's social consciousness and his business sense reflected influences that went back to his youth in Springfield, Illinois, where he was born in 1862, not far from the house of Abraham Lincoln. Young Julius had a happy childhood. His father worked as the managing partner of a large local dry goods business, savvy enough to sell uniforms to the Union Army during the Civil War and commemorative buttons when Lincoln was assassinated. The Rosenwalds were prominent members of Springfield's small Jewish community. They encountered little overt prejudice because of religion, but biographers have noted that they were aware of their minority status in a town that was overwhelmingly Protestant.

In part because of these roots, Rosenwald always maintained close ties to the temple, though he was not particularly spiritual, and religion influenced his life greatly. When he moved to Chicago he became a leading member of the Sinai Congregation on the city's South Side. Sinai was the most important reform congregation in Chicago, so reformed, in fact, that it held services on Sundays. The congregation was headed by Rabbi Emil Hirsch, renowned at that time as a drafter of the Pittsburgh Platform, a famous document that did much to define Reform Judaism in America. The Platform, published in 1885, stressed the necessity for Jews to "participate in the great task of modern times, to solve on the basis of justice and righteousness the problems presented by the contrasts and evils of the present organization of society."

In the 1920s, the era of American robber barons was not long past. Speculation and greed were widespread. Yet Rosenwald surrounded himself with friends and associates who strongly believed that American society could be improved. One important influence on his life was Julian Mack, a Chicago lawyer, a Sinai member, and later a prominent judge on the federal bench. Mack was an early supporter of Jane Addams. He founded Chicago's first juvenile court, directly across the street from Hull House. Mack's influence drew Rosenwald into a number of charities; Mack even took the Sears president, a staunch Republican, to hear a speech by labor activist Grace Abbott. Rosenwald did not approve of Abbott's radical unionism, but it was typical of his tolerance and courtesy that after the meeting he instructed his chauffeur to drive Abbott to her next commitment that evening, which was a rally of striking garment workers.

Another important influence on Rosenwald's career was Paul Sachs, head of the investment bank of Goldman, Sachs & Company. Sachs and Rosenwald became acquainted when they were both young businessmen in New York and haunted vaudeville theaters together. Sachs remained in New York but made frequent trips to Chicago to arrange financing for Sears, Roebuck. When together, they would quickly finish their business and then start in on their real interests, which revolved around the social issues of the day. They discussed social work. They discussed the role of the philanthropist. And they agreed wholeheartedly on one particular point: The most important problem in America was progress for African Americans.

Through Sachs, Rosenwald was introduced to the work of Booker T. Washington, and after reading Washington's autobiography, Rosenwald sought a meeting with the black educator. The two men formed a close personal relationship; Rosenwald loved to tell Washington's personal saga, of how he was born a slave, learned to read against all odds and traveled on foot from his home in West Virginia to enroll at Hampton Institute in Virginia, over 200 miles away.

Rosenwald's relationship with Washington inspired him to begin the program that would make him one of America's most famous philanthropists. It was to fund the construction of new schools for black children throughout the South. This program, like many initiated by Rosenwald, was based on the condition that his contribution be matched by funds from other sources. By the time Rosenwald died in 1932 he had given $5 million for the program, leading to the construction of over 5,000 schools.

ROSENWALD'S LAST AND MOST AMBITIOUS project was the Museum of Science and Industry. He had never before promised $3 million in a single pledge. Never was the need to assemble widespread support for a single undertaking so formidable. Yet plans for the Rosenwald Industrial Museum, as it was called, took form immediately, mostly because of Rosenwald himself. His influence with politicians was effective. His manner with the press was uncommonly deft. He knew who was truly powerful in the world of business, and he enlisted the influential more quickly and effectively than any other man might have done.

Rosenwald's campaign for a new museum began quite naturally with the Commercial Club of Chicago, whose roster was a short list of Chicago's wealthiest and most powerful men. Years before, the Commercial Club had commissioned Daniel Burnham to create the famous *Plan of Chicago* of 1909. "Make no little plans," Burnham had exhorted at the time. Over the years the club grew partial to big plans, and the Museum was certainly one. When Rosenwald broached the idea with Commercial Club members in 1926, there was a positive response. Before a formal announcement was made, they quietly formed a Museum Committee to study the proposal. This committee was the core of the Museum's first board of trustees.

Rosenwald—no egotist—made sure this group included men nearly as powerful as himself. Among them were the chief executive officers of Illinois Bell Telephone, Illinois Central Railroad, First National Bank and other large Chicago corporations. It was a group, moreover, that understood technology and would certainly approve of a museum to promote it. "It is education in a new form," declared Sewell Avery, president of U.S. Gypsum Company (later of Montgomery Ward) and head of the Museum Committee. He spoke of a place with "never a moment of boredom, nor a hint of the tedium that often comes with book learning." What Avery and more than a dozen other Commercial Club members envisioned were locomotives with moving parts, printing presses clattering, large models of modern steel bridges and perhaps even a full-size coal mine.

Another member of the committee, Charles Piez of the Illinois Manufacturers Association, stressed the social utility of such a museum. It could aid in the training of "young men who plan to become prosperous workers in modern industrial plants," Piez said. An industrial school might be opened as part of the Museum. "Industry must find a substitute for the old practice of apprenticeship." Another Commercial Club member at the time was Rufus Dawes, a Chicago banker and brother of the former vice president of the United States,

In 1929, members of the Museum Committee of the Commercial
Club of Chicago met with Julius Rosenwald (seated left) and Oskar von
Miller (seated right) of the Deutsches Museum, which served as a
model for the Chicago project. Standing behind Rosenwald and von Miller
are (left to right) W. R. Abbott, Leo F. Wormser, Harold Swift, Rufus C.
Dawes and Sewell L. Avery.

Charles Dawes. Rufus Dawes, just then becoming involved in plans for a second great world's fair in Chicago, was likewise intrigued. "Rosenwald's gen-
erosity is matched only by his discrimination," he said.

ALTHOUGH THE INITIAL DISCUSSIONS about the Museum were held
in secret, Rosenwald rightly assumed that word of the project would leak out,
which it quickly did, because Chicago had hotly competitive newspapers. With
that in mind, the philanthropist promptly left town. It was ostensibly a family
vacation—to Munich, Vienna and elsewhere—but Rosenwald was well aware
that it would have a secondary effect. That was its news value as Rosenwald
and his family made a tour of Europe's industrial museums. Chicago news-

rooms would catch wind of the story and put their vaunted foreign correspondents on Rosenwald's trail. Rosenwald had left copies of his itinerary behind; he knew that European datelines would give stories about the new museum added importance.

He did not make himself hard to find. While in Vienna, he spoke with the *Chicago Tribune*'s Floyd Gibbons, who reported that Rosenwald was visiting the Deutsches Museum in Munich and the Technisches Museum in Vienna. They were large and exciting institutions, Rosenwald told Gibbons, but there was no reason why America shouldn't have something equally impressive. "I would like every young growing mind in Chicago to be able to see working models, visualizing developments in machines and processes which have been built by the greatest industrial nation in the world," which was of course the United States.

Days later, in Paris, Rosenwald stopped at the office of the *Chicago Daily News* and its correspondent John Gunther (who later gained fame for his *Inside* books such as *Inside Europe* and *Inside U.S.A.*). Rosenwald told Gunther about his visit in Munich with Dr. Oskar von Miller, the founder and director emeritus of the Deutsches Museum. Von Miller, then 70, had been Thomas Edison's protégé and his representative in Germany, as well as a prominent civil engineer in that country, before founding the Deutsches Museum. Originally housed in an old army barracks on the Main River, the museum had since moved to larger quarters, mostly because of von Miller's ability to convince all sectors of German industry to contribute models, machines, expertise and money to a museum that would become one of the most beloved in Germany.

Rosenwald, normally a man of few words, was remarkably talkative with Gunther. "We saw cross-section exhibits of mines of all kinds, of canal construction, of applied mechanics, of airplanes and dirigibles, of U-boats and battle ships. We saw, too, not only the models but the machines themselves—airplane engines, derricks, blast furnaces, as well as every sort of industrial application of devices in metallurgy, physics, chemistry and geology. In particular, I remember a beautiful model called 'Planetarium,' which with magnificent precision, demonstrates the movement of our world in the solar system."

The public was clearly intrigued, and other reporters soon dug around for stories of their own. For them, Rosenwald took to repeating the "real" story of how the Museum was conceived. It had all begun in 1922 on a previous family trip to Munich. After visiting with their German cousins, of which there were many, the Rosenwalds made more or less obligatory tours of the city's many cultural institutions. They were naturally impressed by the galleries devoted to art and antiquities, but were never truly excited until they got to the Deutsches Museum. It was there that the Rosenwald's youngest child, William, then 14, showed limitless wonder at the cranks and switches that operated engines and even an X-ray machine. He particularly loved the coal mine in the museum's sprawling basement. His son came away, Rosenwald said, with quite an education. It was then that he decided Chicago needed a place like it. "In the Munich museum there is none of the 'hands off' attitude which marks practically every museum exhibit in America," Rosenwald told another newsman.

When Rosenwald returned to America and readied himself for the formal announcement of his plan, he left the dozens of essential details to his personal attorney, Leo Wormser. Wormser's enthusiasm for the project was indispensable as he became both administrator and promoter of the new museum. Wormser made certain that the Museum Committee was always well informed. On the day of the announcement in August 1926, he arranged for the current director of the Deutsches Museum, Dr. Albert Koch, to be present. For the benefit of the press, and with the help of an interpreter, Koch expressed surprise that America lacked an industrial museum such as the one they had in Munich. He heartily endorsed the idea of a museum for Chicago and even suggested that his museum had duplicate models to donate.

It also fell to Wormser to secure the support of the South Park Commissioners, because the Palace of Fine Arts was on park land in Jackson Park, and they controlled the $5 million in revenue bonds that would be necessary to rebuild the structure. This effort, too, was successful, and Wormser even convinced Commission president Edward J. Kelly to pose with Rosenwald, Koch and others in front of the building. The photo ran in the papers the day after the project was announced.

In many ways the success of the Museum of Science and Industry was a tribute to Leo Wormser's persuasiveness. In a progress report to the Commercial Club some months later, his remarks, as always, resonated completely with the capitalists. He took pains, for instance, to describe a future exhibit on transportation which would include, in all likelihood, cross sections of roads as they were engineered in ancient Rome. But the focus would be entirely up to date. "Today, when we of Illinois are witnessing a political career building largely upon the slogan 'hard roads,'" he said, in reference to a less-than-respectable Illinois official then in ascendance, "it may be interesting to inquire whether we have really made any improvement in the art of road building."

Rosenwald and Wormser also took extra steps to cultivate political powers. In one case, to strengthen the resolve of the South Park Commissioners, they offered to send the group on a grand tour of Europe to see the great industrial museums for themselves. Rosenwald's alliance with the park commission was essential, and particularly important was the support of Kelly, an immensely powerful man who would later become mayor of Chicago. The offer was accepted, and before leaving for Europe, Kelly expressed his gratitude with well-placed remarks to the press. "The whole German nation is benefited intellectually and Munich is benefited commercially" by the Deutsches Museum, he said. Chicago should have one like it. "A boy visiting a show is inspired by what he sees. He starts making things at home instead of stealing autos and running wild."

The European trip of Kelly and the commissioners was arranged very carefully indeed. The entourage was greeted in Munich, Vienna, Paris, London and a number of other cities by local political officials. In Rome they had a private audience with the Pope. Kelly did not write home frequently during the month-long trip, but he was obviously impressed by what he saw. "Some trip. Some museums," he scrawled on a card posted to Leo Wormser. When Kelly returned on the ocean liner *Olympic* he was met by reporters in New York, and when he got off the train in Chicago he was greeted by the press again. Kelly assured everyone he was thrilled to be back, that Chicago looked better than any old European city to him. But the trip had been highly worthwhile. He had determined that the idea for an industrial museum was excellent. The Palace of Fine Arts as a site was ideal. The project would be expensive, Kelly warned, more than previous estimates. But funds would be raised, and Chicago would have "the greatest industrial museum in the world."

Politically, all was well.

THE QUIET JULIUS ROSENWALD knew that things were not as simple as they sounded. Political support was necessary, but the Museum was a project of massive scale and would require substantially more backing. It would need the goodwill of industry—which seemed to be coming. It also needed the support of educational institutions, and early on Rosenwald got the immediate endorsement of the University of Chicago's president, Max Mason. Mason promised complete cooperation, and delivered it in the form of esteemed scientists who made important contributions in the critical early years of the Museum. Another supporter was William J. Bogan, Chicago's school superintendent. Bogan, too, was interested in ways the schools might interact with the Museum, which he said would have "a far reaching influence educationally for the workers, inventors and citizens of Chicago for all years to come."

Helpful words also came from powerful figures outside Chicago. George Vincent, president of the Rockefeller Foundation, wrote several enthusiastic letters of support to the organizers of the Museum, though he warned that the ambition to be the "largest in the world" might be self-defeating. "There is great danger in magnification of the Museum," Vincent wrote. "The Munich Museum is, if anything, too large. The important thing is quality and not quantity." Wormser wrote back to Vincent, a longtime acquaintance of Rosenwald, that they agreed. The promise of mammoth size was local political bluster and "sponsored by none of us."

Rosenwald and Wormser were keenly sensitive to any and all obstacles, paying particular attention in those early months to "competitor" museums. In magnanimous moments, Rosenwald declared that Chicago must cooperate fully with the similar museums being planned in New York and Washington, because they all had much to offer one another. Yet he was extremely quick to note when those projects, as well as another being planned by Henry Ford in Detroit, got national publicity and the Chicago museum did not. Public relations were a serious and constant concern of Rosenwald and Wormser. They briefed each other prior to any contact with the press. They saved and analyzed clippings on any subject related to museums. And although cooperation in all endeavors was to be encouraged, there were limits. "We must not overlook the inroads that these other projects may make upon our efforts to obtain exhibits," Wormser wrote.

There was yet another project that gave the Rosenwald forces cause for concern. It was A Century of Progress, the world's fair planned for Chicago in 1933, the city's 100th anniversary. This would be a huge public exposition of modern technology, which was to open at approximately the same time as the Museum. Its theme, too, was science and industry. It, too, was being promoted to private industries, foreign governments and whoever else might provide colorful and impressive exhibits. Open jealousy over A Century of Progress was never voiced by the Museum's organizers, but Wormser was privately astonished when its aims were published and bore striking similarity to those already stated by the Museum. The fair would be "an exposition of the service of science to society and of the benefit to humanity brought about by this scientific and industrial development."

Fortunately, the Museum and the fair were quick to realize that cooperation would benefit everyone concerned. Some aspects of planning, they concluded, could be done jointly. Exhibits could be shared. Visitors to Chicago could come to both. As a result, strong ties were formed between the planners of Rosenwald's museum and A Century of Progress. The outcome was a happy one for the Museum. When the fair closed, its Hall of Science—with dozens of exhibits on basic principles from electromagnetism to the chemistry of petroleum—became a centerpiece of the Museum of Science and Industry. Other exhibits from A Century of Progress ultimately came in as well, from Bell Telephone's *Oscar*, which created "acoustical illusions," to the spectacular Piccard gondola when it was finally retired from flight.

ANOTHER QUESTION THAT CONCERNED the organizers of the new museum was its name. This became a complicated issue. From the beginning, most people assumed it would be the Rosenwald Industrial Museum, which was only fitting. But the donor was vacillating on this point. Only in rare instances had Rosenwald allowed his name used on the scores of buildings he had funded. Aside from his natural modesty, his often-stated belief was that such an honor might oblige his heirs to continue support after his death.

With the Museum, however, there is evidence that Rosenwald would have welcomed the tribute. "From a remark Julius made to me one day I believe he wants this museum to be a permanent monument to his name," wrote Frank Wetmore, chairman of the First National Bank. But for odd reasons, drops of poison seeped in. A news report in the *Chicago Daily News* stated that Chairman Kelly of the park commissioners did not favor Rosenwald's name on the building. There is evidence that Kelly was misquoted, but talk continued. Some said, sotto voce, that the Palace of Fine Arts, and the Museum, belonged to the people of Chicago. Rosenwald's millions would pay only for its contents. There was suspicion among some that anti-Semitism was behind this sentiment.

As the issue unfolded, the board did select the "Rosenwald Industrial Museum" as its formal name as they prepared papers of incorporation. Their vote was unanimous. Then, only hours later, Wormser received a wire from Rosenwald, who was vacationing in the Poconos. He said he had considered the question and had decided that the "Industrial Museum of Chicago" was preferable. Wormser quickly polled the board. All assumed that Rosenwald was being unnecessarily modest. Papers for the Rosenwald Museum were drawn up as voted.

Rosenwald persisted, however. More clearly than the rest, the philanthropist foresaw that $3 million was enough only to start a museum and that community support would be needed to sustain it. So he dashed off a letter to Wormser: "If I were not convinced that it will in the long run be prejudicial I would have been delighted to have my name connected with it as you may readily imagine. If no name is used it will belong to the people." It was an order this time. Wormser and the board complied and changed the name. For years afterward, the public continued to call it the Rosenwald Museum, out of affection or habit. According to the donor's wishes it was renamed the Museum of Science and Industry, followed by a coda: "Founded by Julius Rosenwald."

By all lights the decision was a good one. It assured a broader base of support from scholars, companies, schools, and even governments from around the world. Because of this support, it was destined to become the world's largest industrial museum, and one of the most famous museums of any kind in the United States. For this it owed much to its quiet but clear-eyed founder.

THREE

The Museum's "Technical Ascent"

For the Museum of Science and Industry to succeed, support from many quarters of Chicago was essential. The plan required more than a great palace and even more than Julius Rosenwald's $3 million. Politicians would need to make public funds available. Private enterprise would need to contribute machines and models. Teachers and universities would need to be involved to help explain what it all meant.

The Museum's role would be to assemble the great story of technology. The story would involve agriculture, transportation, electricity and dozens of other industries—and illustrate the rise of Western civilization itself. Everyone involved in the project agreed that if the saga could be told anywhere, it could be and must be told in Chicago. It was equally clear that if the Museum were to realize this goal, it would need an extraordinary person to direct it. But no one knew who it would be.

The board of trustees, powerful men themselves, knew very well that grand visions needed skilled organizers. Thus, the board's first priority was to make a list of the qualifications required for an executive director and to conduct a serious search to find him. Because there were no major industrial museums in the United States at that time, it would be difficult. Obvious candidates were not apt to emerge. The right person might come from industry or perhaps from academia. It would be a national search, even international. Finding a man (a woman was never considered) with suitable technical and executive skills, the trustees knew, would take effort and time.

At the same time, the workload of Museum business was growing enormously. No sooner was the Museum announced than Rosenwald's office was besieged with not only congratulations but suggestions, advice, solicitations and other offers. Scholars, inventors, designers, sales representatives and more than a few hucksters got their letters to the inner sanctum at Sears. The storm of interest in Rosenwald's museum was encouraging, but it also made matters chaotic. The new museum had apparently struck a public nerve, and as a result, résumés and proposals, some helpful, others strange, flowed in.

Museum mail in the early months included letters from Richard L. Crampton, former manager of the Illinois Bankers Association, who wrote lengthily about a previous study for an industrial museum in Chicago. He noted that the study had envisioned such an institution in Grant Park, closer to Chicago's center of business. Should the Rosenwald group ever reconsider the Jackson Park site, Crampton was quick to offer his services "as broker in the matter, as I am now interested in Industrial surveys, Financing and Real Estate for special clients."

The man may have been fishing for business, but he also appeared sincerely interested in "the important problem of Economic Education in the United States." Crampton obviously had given the idea considerable thought, writing that the previous study had called for exhibits "departing somewhat from the traditional rather static museum methods in order to vitalize the accomplishments of industry." This sounded much like the museum of machines and motion that Rosenwald had in mind. Crampton added that such a museum might also have "commercial marts for the exhibit of related products and equipment," rentable space, in other words, that could raise money and sustain the institution financially. For good or ill, the latter point was never considered by most of the trustees. They conceived of something closer to an "art institute of industry"—more scholarly than commercial—with strangely little concern, at least in the beginning, for who would pay to keep it going.

Another letter came from an inventor named David Todd, of Waverley, Massachusetts, who wrote to suggest that a planetarium would be an excellent addition to the new museum. Todd began with congratulations to Rosenwald for conceiving such a worthy project. He went on to recommend that before Rosenwald's architects got too far along they should add a dome with a screen on the inside. As luck would have it, Todd himself had developed a planetarium projector—an improvement on other such devices on the market—and would be happy to install one in Chicago. In fact, this idea appealed to Rosenwald, as the planetarium at the Deutsches Museum attracted huge crowds. He finally decided against it, however, leaving the subject of heavenly bodies to another cultural institution in Chicago, the Adler Planetarium, which Rosenwald's son-in-law Max Adler was already planning.

Other suggestions for the new museum strayed wider from the mark. One interested party insisted that Rosenwald's museum should include an exhibit of bird's nests, and that Rosenwald might do very well to finance a collecting expedition to China, where some such specimens were edible and regarded as delicacies. Leo Wormser replied gracefully that the writer was probably thinking of the wrong museum. Still another letter came from a New York enterprise called The Psychotechnicum with a product called the Konzentrator. This bizarre device was worn on the head like a crown. "It revitalizes the neurons, the bi-polar brain nerve cells; develops a more receptive more retentive memory no course of training can procure, and helps to concentrate thought." Using the Konzentrator, the letter promised, "is like the effect of focusing the rays of the sun through a lens, upon a focal point—*the burning point.*" It was unclear whether The Psychotechnicum wanted the Museum to consider their miracle of science for an exhibit or whether they believed the trustees and curators could profit from its use. The cost was $10 for each copy of the device. The Museum was not seriously tempted.

TO FIND AN EXECUTIVE to deal with these and hundreds of other immediate details, the trustees undertook a methodical search. Wormser began with letters to people of influence to ask for their help. Among them was Rosenwald's friend George Vincent of the Rockefeller Foundation, who agreed that the directorship was "a one man job . . . . That is, the director ought to have so thorough a grasp of the fundamental idea of the museum that he could assume complete responsibility . . . namely that a relatively young, well-trained and imaginative professor of mechanical engineering in some good engineering school would be the right type of executive." Above all, Vincent said, the director should be practical, not a misty "educator" who might be less familiar with real inventions, working machines and people who go to museums.

Rosenwald himself thought that the Museum really needed an established businessman who could actually preside over the board of trustees with authority, and not just take orders from it. The University of Chicago had such a man in Harold Swift, president of Union Stock Yards. Stanley Field, a relative of Marshall Field, had a similar role at the Field Museum. Most men of this type were probably spoken for, Rosenwald concluded, but he reiterated the need for a strong and entrepreneurial executive director.

Various candidates emerged, then disappeared. Wormser contacted Dr. Samuel Stratton, president of Massachusetts Institute of Technology, about the position. Stratton showed no interest in leaving MIT, but he did offer the name of Dr. F. C. Brown, an engineer who had worked closely with Stratton when both were at the U.S. Bureau of Standards. Brown was currently working for New York's Museum of the Peaceful Arts, and when contacted seemed willing to move to Chicago, where plans for the Museum clearly were farther along than those in New York. Ultimately, Brown's ties to the East were too strong and his candidacy fizzled.

As months passed in 1927, the search grew increasingly urgent. Starkly different opinions on the subject of an executive director began to emerge. Charles Piez, for example, favored a powerful board of trustees with a director hired primarily to "fetch and carry." Piez ultimately deferred to Rosenwald's wishes for a strong man at the helm. Nevertheless, the relationship between the Museum's board of trustees and its executive director would remain a troubled one for years to come.

THE NAME OF WALDEMAR KAEMPFFERT came up on several occasions during this process. It was first mentioned in a letter from William Dubilier, an inventor and president of the Dubilier Condenser and Radio Corporation in New York, with whom the trustees corresponded. Kaempffert had interesting credentials. He was the science editor of the *New York Times*, and had formerly been managing editor of *Scientific American* and *Popular Science* magazines. He was also author of *A Popular History of American Invention* and had a well-known gift for making complex technical subjects understandable. Shortly after learning about Kaempffert, Wormser bought a copy of Kaempffert's *Popular History* and took it with him on a trip to the East Coast. As fate would have it, the attorney read the first chapter, "From Stephens to the Twentieth Century Limited—The Story of American Railroading," while he himself was riding the Twentieth Century from Chicago to New York. And he noted with satisfaction that many important inventions described in the chapter, such as Pullman coaches and refrigerated boxcars, had been developed in no place other than Chicago. Kaempffert's stock rose, and over a period of months he emerged as the prime candidate to be the man the Museum needed.

The courtship was polite and restrained. It began with Wormser writing Kaempffert primarily for insight into the qualifications of another candidate, a German engineer and protégé of Oskar von Miller at the Deutsches Museum, Dr. Max von Recklinghausen. Kaempffert, himself of German parentage, gave a cautious assessment of Recklinghausen, but he added that no one found for the Chicago position was likely to measure up to von Miller. "As a director of such museums, Dr. von Miller certainly outshines all his competitors," Kaempffert wrote. "Von Miller has tried to make it live. Most of my life has been spent in popularizing science and engineering and I know of no finer work in this field than what Dr. von Miller is doing in Munich." Kaempffert was well aware that he too was being considered for the post. Still, he freely offered the names of other potential candidates, including Professor Vladimir Karapetoff of Cornell and Dr. E. E. Slossen of the National Research Council. (Slossen was also a science writer with "literary ability of a high order.") Kaempffert further warned that the right man for the job would be in high demand. As Wormser undoubtedly knew, other cities were planning industrial museums. They were looking for the same kind of individual Chicago was.

Friendly correspondence continued. Wormser replied that Karapetoff and

Slossen probably lacked "organizing ability." Kaempffert wrote back, enclosing a clip from the English science journal *Nature* with a two-page advertisement for the directorship of a small science and technology museum being planned in Cambridge. The notice described this institution in detail and then concluded: "Thus arises the need for a technique to utilize and develop the child's native curiosity in the way the wheels go around—his interest for instance in mud and water and his pleasure in messing about—in such a way as, in the long run, to obtain the maximum conversion of these drives into a controllable instrument of organized thought." Despite the run-on prose, Kaempffert's missive made instructive points, one of which was that Kaempffert himself well understood the mission that the Chicago organizers had in mind. Because the trustees were getting impatient—1927 was nearly over—Wormser thanked Kaempffert for his continued interest. He also said that he had other business coming up in New York. Might they please meet? They did, and the subject of the position in Chicago was quickly addressed. Kaempffert was interested.

Rash action was against the nature of everyone involved. The trustees ran what amounted to a lengthy background check on Kaempffert. They turned up nothing that disqualified him. On the contrary, most references gave him glowing reports. Colleagues at the *New York Times* regarded the editor as "an unusually intelligent, well-informed and cultivated person." George Vincent, who knew him as well, wrote that "his experience and interests have a wide range. They are predominantly scientific but extend to art, music and drama." A partner in a Manhattan advertising agency, a former employer of Kaempffert, remembered that nearly a decade before, the candidate had handled publicity for the New York visit of Guglielmo Marconi, the Italian inventor of wireless communications. Kaempffert's work on the account was uncommonly successful. "He had a gift of putting a dull scientific speech of Marconi's on the first page of all the newspapers."

Pro-Kaempffert forces on the board grew—one member called him "a great find." A single dissenting trustee, however, was W. Rufus Abbott, president of Illinois Bell Telephone Company. Abbott believed that Kaempffert simply lacked proper administrative skills. He was concerned that the newspaperman was trained only to report on science and had never practiced it himself, and furthermore, that a reporter "might be disposed to exploit the startling and bizarre rather than the ultimate aim of science." Abbott gently lobbied the other trustees for a continuation of the search. In fact, suspicions that Kaempffert was a sensationalist were well off the mark, and Abbott was overruled. But his misgivings about administrative ability were not forgotten, least of all by Abbott himself.

WALDEMAR KAEMPFFERT WAS KEENLY INTERESTED in an industrial museum and had been for years. As a dedicated popularizer of science, he had traveled to Europe many times, had visited the great industrial museums, and shared the enthusiasm for a major institution of that type in America. Still, the closer he got to being offered the position of executive director of the Chicago project, the more lukewarm he seemed to become. In truth, it was not for lack of interest. Kaempffert was a very busy journalist. With technology making important news nearly every week in engineering, aviation, medicine and many other areas, his attention was more than fully occupied. On several occasions that autumn, Kaempffert was invited to Chicago to meet with the trustees but was obliged to send his regrets because of other commitments. It was not until January 1928 that he finally got on the train for the trip to Chicago. There he enjoyed what all reported was a smooth and uncommonly successful interview. He was invited to meet with the Commercial Club. Still uncertain about taking the Chicago position, he begged off such a coming-out party. He had to get back to New York.

Even after Leo Wormser came to Kaempffert with an offer, the candidate delayed. This was bewildering to the trustees, and some suggested that they refocus the search elsewhere. But it was Rosenwald himself who counseled patience. The position had gone unfilled too long already. Kaempffert was probably the best candidate, and he should be given the time needed to reach his decision. Finally in late February, a letter came from New York. Kaempffert wanted to accept the position, but only if several conditions were met. One was freedom from political pressure in hiring curators and developing exhibits. Another was permission to sail for Europe almost immediately to make a careful study of the industrial museums there. "Without some period of European study it is possible that mistakes may be made which it would be difficult to correct without considerable expense." As for salary, he wanted $20,000 a year, "commensurate with the dignity, importance, and responsibilities of a position which is regarded as one of the highest that a man can be called upon to fill."

The matter was referred to Rosenwald. "I like the enthusiasm he manifests for the job and the evident grasp of the needs," Rosenwald wrote from his vacation hotel in Palm Beach. "The salary matter seems to me entirely fair for a start. It will give opportunity for increase when we get under way."

The Museum had an executive director.

WALDEMAR KAEMPFFERT HIT THE GROUND RUNNING. Though he remained in New York for several months to finish his work at the *New York Times*, he traveled to Chicago in April 1928 for the announcement of his appointment and to address the Commercial Club. In that speech, he elaborated on his ideas for Chicago's new museum. At the Blackstone Hotel that evening, he struck quickly at the core of the club's concern. "Why do we have an industrial museum?" he asked rhetorically. "Look around you in the city of Chicago. Wonderful tall buildings. Wonderful railways. Great industries on

Waldemar Kaempffert had been science editor of the *New York Times* and one of America's leading technology writers when he arrived in Chicago to become the first executive director of the Museum of Science and Industry. He ultimately clashed with trustees and resigned, but in little more than two years he left a deep impression on the Museum's identity.

every hand. As the ancient Greeks used to say, 'How do you get that way?' Well you did not get that way by yourself. You built on something that went before." The men in attendance—whose power clearly relied on the march of industry—could only nod in assent.

As Kaempffert went on he described a museum that would tell one of the greatest stories of all time—a story that had not yet been told to an American audience in an adequate manner. "There is an evolution in civilization as there is in biology. The world has been going on and on. It is a play. The curtain arose thousands of years ago. The last act has not been played and it will not be played. . . . The chief object of this museum, as I see it, is to become a great educational force in teaching us just how the great industrial drama began, how we evolved."

These were all welcome words. The public mind at that time had been casting industry and commerce in an unfortunately negative light. Popular literature—the novels of Theodore Dreiser and Upton Sinclair, for example—portrayed Chicago itself as a city of exploitation and disease. Sinclair Lewis' Babbitt, the quintessential businessman, was completely trapped by small-minded and crooked interests. But now here was Waldemar Kaempffert, himself an esteemed writer from New York, taking a grand and farsighted view, and with plans for an immense museum to prove it. "We want to take you through perhaps ten centuries, twenty centuries, in an afternoon," he said. "And when you come out of that museum you will have a feeling that you have been part of a great industrial organism."

Kaempffert then switched off the lights and began a slide presentation with dozens of photographs. The pictures came mostly from the Deutsches Museum. One view was of an exhibit of bicycles, from the high-wheelers and "boneshakers of our youth" to the modern "safety bicycle," Kaempffert said. It was accompanied by a chart comparing the distance covered by each bicycle with a single revolution of the crank. "What better evidence do you want of the strides that have been made in the evolution of this sort of transportation?" The director went on to show flying machines, from early gliders to the type of modern planes then crossing the Atlantic. Human flight was one of the major chapters in the history of technology. The Museum would tell the story. Kaempffert even revealed his determination (later thwarted) to have the Wright brothers' first flying machine, the *Kitty Hawk*, as a centerpiece.

The Chicago museum would also employ, and hopefully improve upon, many educational techniques pioneered at the Deutsches Museum, such as "sectioned" machines, dissected to reveal the moving parts inside. Kaempffert showed how a locomotive was equipped with small electric motors to demonstrate the workings of valves, pistons and driving wheels. A Bessemer converter could likewise illustrate the process of making steel—with lights trained on the boiling stream of air bubbles that oxidized and removed impurities from the pig-iron mass. These were the "masterpieces of science and engineering," Kaempffert said, around which the new Museum would be built.

For Commercial Club members who might take a more hardheaded view of the enterprise, the new executive director pointed out that Munich's museum drew 900,000 visitors yearly, and Chicago, a larger city, could be expected to do better still. Few people who heard Kaempffert's speech that night doubted that he was the right messenger. "Contrary to the fear that has been expressed by some novelists that we will be dominated by the machine," Kaempffert promised, "we are living in the most comfortable age that ever lived."

ALTHOUGH KAEMPFFERT WAS OBVIOUSLY ADEPT at plucking at the entrepreneurial, quintessentially American heartstrings of his audience, the first thing he did after his appointment and his speech in Chicago was embark for Europe. His principal destinations were the Deutsches Museum in Munich and the Technisches Museum in Vienna, where he spent nearly two months and learned many detailed lessons of museum management.

At both Munich and Vienna, for example, he was intrigued, as well as confounded, by efforts to classify the many branches of science and technology in a neat and comprehensible scheme. If progress was evolutionary—as Kaempffert was convinced it was—how did one scientific discovery lead to the next? How could inventions in transportation, metals, steam power and electricity be contained in a single script? Where did science end and industry begin, or vice versa? What about textiles and agriculture? Optics and astronomy?

In his frequent letters from Europe, and in detailed reports made later, Kaempffert described the organization of the European museums. He noted, for example, that Vienna divided mechanics and engineering into three historical groups: In ancient times people were dependent on muscle and wind. The Middle Ages saw the introduction of heat engines. The modern age brought the miracles of electricity. Also in Vienna, large and impressive models left no doubt about many crucial leaps forward in technology. One exhibit, for example, featured two mechanical pumps placed side by side. The one built in 1870 labored noisily. The one from 1928 was small and efficient. This was obviously evolution.

The Deutsches Museum was vaster than the Technisches Museum, with many more divisions, and its organization was thought out in extreme detail. With German discipline, visitors marched sequentially through the museum, from hall to hall—from thermodynamics to electricity, from mining to metallurgy. While this approach was highly effective for Munich, Kaempffert wondered about Chicago. "An American may object that this system of compulsory guidance would be accepted only in Germany," he wrote, "but that it would never meet the requirements of the United States where every free-born American considers it his natural privilege to disregard the best laid plans of librarians, school-principals and police departments." Telling the story of science and industry, in other words, was no simple undertaking.

Kaempffert, who spoke German like a native, also met with architects on his trip. Among other things, he concluded that Chicago must "allow for some method whereby aeroplanes weighing as much as four tons can be suspended from the central hall of our main building." He was concerned that the architects in Chicago were making decisions in his absence. The design of the building, in fact, would be anything but simple. In another letter to Wormser and the trustees, Kaempffert warned that planning the interior too early could lead to unhappiness later.

"It is freely confessed in Vienna and Munich," Kaempffert wrote, "that there was much futile floundering about in endeavoring to indicate to architects just what provisions must be made. An art museum can be planned with the utmost attention to detail, simply because pictures and statues vary in size within rather narrow limits. . . . With a technical museum it is otherwise. Exhibits may range in size from a pin to full-sized windmills and objects even larger." Even as the Deutsches Museum was being constructed, Kaempffert related, requirements had changed. The decision to include a planetarium was made midstream. Plans for the German museum's famous half-scale coal mine had changed so many times that "it had to be tucked away in odd spaces."

There were other ecstasies and agonies in Europe. During his stay in Vienna, Kaempffert was informed that Julius Rosenwald had been awarded the Grosses Auszeichen (high decoration) of the Austrian Republic, primarily for $5,000 he had given the Technisches Museum in an hour of grave need. Reports of this honor were promptly published in America and Europe, and its prestige actually opened several doors for Kaempffert in his travels.

The press could be troublesome as well. When a *Chicago Tribune* reporter caught up with Kaempffert in Paris, the director gladly gave him an interview. Unfortunately the article that resulted, focusing on atomic science, was a complete fiasco. "Science may some day solve the greatest problem—the disintegration of the atom," Kaempffert was quoted as saying. "But it is quite likely to blow up the universe in the process." Kaempffert wrote back to Wormser that this misrepresentation was "something appalling." Journalists were indispensable, of course, but also dangerous.

SHORTLY AFTER RETURNING HOME, Kaempffert compiled his thoughts on industrial museums in a long article for *Scientific Monthly*, a piece that quickly became a manifesto for the Chicago project. In "The Technical Ascent of Man," as the article was entitled, he stressed that society must not take technological progress for granted. "When Giotto finished a picture all Florence was jubilant and stopped work to celebrate the completion of a masterpiece," he wrote. "It is perhaps asking too much that a city declare a holiday and rejoice at the discovery of X-rays, but it is not too much to expect an intelligent public to discover what the rays mean to mankind as they find wider and wider application."

Ultimately, Waldemar Kaempffert's tenure as director of the Museum of Science and Industry was all too short. Little more than two years later, the political stresses of Chicago and the administrative strains of the job were to send him back to his former position at the *New York Times*. Nevertheless, Kaempffert's directorship set the stage for exciting new ways of understanding technology and human invention. "To a socially tense people relief comes through art, philosophy, religion, arms, or science, depending upon the crucial need of the moment," he wrote in another article. "Horace, Dante, Shakespeare,

Voltaire, Bach, Newton, Watt, Morse, Bell, Edison, and Marconi must be regarded as fuses that blow and enable society to short circuit itself by following the lines of least resistance." Inventors, like artists, were dependent on what came before, and there was something inevitable, if not predictable, about progress. "The idea that an idea flashes from the brain and gives the world a sudden, fresh impulse, must be dismissed."

Kaempffert made very big plans. And in the time he spent imagining and designing the Museum of Science and Industry, there was not a hint of doubt that he would succeed. The *Chicago Tribune* reported that his very appointment had brought the planned museum "much closer to reality." The paper regularly covered his pronouncements long before the Museum was ever open. The public was particularly pleased when Kaempffert said he hoped the president of the United States—Herbert Hoover, who was himself an engineer—would come to Chicago to dedicate this important new institution when it was ready.

But that would take five long years. By then, not only was Kaempffert gone, the nation had a new president. The Great Depression had arrived. A raft of practical problems hampered the Museum's lofty plans. Expectations were lowered. Perhaps this was predictable. Kaempffert, after all, had been clear on one point. Progress may be inevitable, but it was often slow and rarely painless.

The old Palace of Fine Arts, originally built of plaster, was reconstructed
piece by piece in limestone to house the Museum of Science and Industry.
The exterior remained a Beaux Arts masterpiece. As the interior took
form in the '30s, it was lauded as one of the finest examples of modern
streamlined architecture in Chicago.

The Palace

As it had for many years, the Palace of Fine Arts sat in dignified ruins on the edge of Jackson Park. It was decayed and turning grey, and there were concerns for its safety, but from a distance it called to mind Chicago's noble past. This was the last major vestige of the World's Columbian Exposition, the sparkling White City of 1893 that drew visitors from everywhere that summer when Chicago was, for the moment at least, the center of the civilized world.

The Palace of Fine Arts also recalled a great blaze that had occurred the following year, when many of the fair's stately pavilions caught fire and were consumed in one convulsive night. It was almost a mystical sight, not altogether tragic because the exposition had concluded successfully and the fire took no lives. The earthly pavilions of the ethereal fair had "gone back to heaven," it was said, and very quickly all traces of the great event were but a memory—all except this one. The Palace of Fine Arts, later called the Fine Arts Building, survived the fire of 1894. That same year it went on to become the Field Museum of Natural History. The Field Museum abandoned it in 1920, and its plaster walls began to crumble. Even in ruins the palace ranked high in the esteem of Chicagoans, who often repeated the assessment of Augustus Saint-Gaudens that its architecture was "unequaled since the Parthenon."

The irony of the Fine Arts Building was that it almost was not built at all. The World's Columbian Exposition of 1893 was conceived to be a show of technical and industrial genius, the raw power behind America's rise—not of the fine arts, which were associated with Europe. But as plans for the mammoth fair took form, Chicago saw the opportunity to take its place at the head of the world's great cities. Thus organizers determined to add painting and sculpture to the mechanical arts in this exposition of man's highest achievements.

Building a palace for the purpose would not be simple. An appropriate site was the first problem, because the fair's central court, the Court of Honor, was already fully planned. An architect also would need to be found, and most of America's leading architects were at that moment occupied with other buildings for the fair. Moreover, Chicago had to soothe the fears of art patrons in Europe, such as Pope Leo XIII, who refused to send art treasures to Chicago without assurance that the gallery built to house them was fireproof.

Yet these were mere practical questions, and the exposition director, Daniel Burnham, was nothing if not a master at resolving matters of this kind. The arts pavilion, he decided, could be located on vacant land across the North Lagoon from the Court of Honor, secure from any inferno (perish the thought) that might rage through other buildings. The structure would receive still greater protection, for unlike most buildings for the fair—steel frames covered with wood and plaster—this one would have a substructure of brick, which was considered effective in resisting fire.

As for choosing an architect, that would require more patience than even Daniel Burnham had initially. In 1891, Burnham's own firm was left without a chief designer when his partner John Wellborn Root died of pneumonia, apparently after a visit to frigid, windswept Jackson Park. With time running short, a young classical architect from Harvard, Charles B. Atwood, was recommended by Eastern colleagues, and Burnham quickly made plans to visit him in New York. Their meeting was planned for the Brunswick Hotel, but when the appointed time came, Atwood was nowhere to be seen. Burnham waited for an hour before leaving to make his train back to Chicago. Then, outside the station, the director was accosted by a breathless young man who said he was Charles Atwood. The Chicagoan was brusque, saying he had a train to catch, that he might communicate with him later, but he was probably going to make other plans. Whatever Burnham's thoughts were on the ride home, he was surprised the following day when Atwood arrived in his office in Chicago. They had an interview and came to terms. Atwood was hired.

In the two years that followed, Atwood designed several other buildings on the exposition grounds, but the Palace of Fine Arts was instantly recognized as his masterpiece. It was a harmonious blend of classical motifs in the Beaux Arts fashion of the day. It included aspects of the Parthenon, with details from the frieze of the Greek original. The caryatids, which were columns in the form of women supporting the building's weight, were modeled after the Erechtheum, also on the Acropolis in Athens. Atwood added domes, unknown to classical architecture until Rome; the largest one was placed over a central hall inside that was 128 feet high. Artists everywhere were excited about Atwood's splendid work. A few cynics noted that it copied a design that a French architect had drawn for the Prix de Rome competition some years before. There were similarities, but in fact Atwood was an immensely skilled and original classicist. When other architects examined his drawings, they searched for violations in proportion. "Confound him," said one. "He is right every time."

TOWARD THE END of the triumphant Columbian Exposition, the Palace of Fine Arts became the subject of a meeting between two prominent Chicagoans, Edward E. Ayer and Marshall Field. Ayer, a Chicago lumberman and armchair anthropologist, asked Field, one of Chicago's wealthiest men, to fund a new museum contemplated to occupy the Atwood building. A museum, Ayer said, would maintain in Chicago many exhibits from the Columbian Exposition and would preserve the Palace of Fine Arts as well. Field appeared reluctant. Ayer countered, riskily, by saying that true immortality did not come to men who sold dry goods—only a museum could etch Field's name in stone. The story is that Field was angered by the remark and threw Ayer out of his office. Upon further reflection, however, he reconsidered. The following day Field wrote a check for $1 million, then the largest single donation ever to a museum.

The Field Columbian Museum, which opened in 1894, would house a great variety of valuable collections. They included anthropological exhibits—pre-Columbian gold, Javanese carvings and countless objects of American Indians and African peoples. There were minerals from the exposition's large and popular exhibits on mining and metallurgy. Other specimens, sent to Chicago from around the world, included oils, gums, resins, fibers, fruits, seeds and grains—these formed the beginnings of the botany department. The Field Museum was quickly successful and established a worldwide reputation. Quite naturally it began planning a move to a new building, one sheathed in stone and not plaster.

In 1920 it completed one, situated on new landfill in Grant Park south of the Loop and built of gleaming white marble. Then discussions began about what to do with the old Palace of Fine Arts. Various plans were made to restore it in some manner. Among them were ideas for a convention hall. But mostly the efforts consisted of committee work and newspaper editorials, with few schemes laid out for financing the restoration. As the old pavilion lay deserted in the years that followed, it grew worn and hollow, but it also became a favorite evening destination for many Chicagoans. "I confess I liked it best in its former semi-ruined state," wrote high-society novelist Arthur Meeker years after it was restored. "The peeling plaster walls reflected in the lagoon had a curious romantic charm."

In 1922, the South Park Commissioners, who had authority over the building, resolved to tear it down. The vote was 3–2. The decision was made, they said, in the interest of public safety. Even as they explained such reasonable motives, rumblings to save it grew louder. Lorado Taft, Chicago's venerable sculptor, stated that it should be a gallery of sculpture and could be as important a museum as the Trocadero of Paris. Businessmen imagined a "great Industrial Art School, with its class rooms and work shops, such as abound in all the industrial centers of Europe," wrote William Pelouze, president of the Association of Arts and Industries. It was enough for park commissioner Edward J. Kelly, one of the two voters against demolition, to stop the bulldozers. He believed that the cause was popular, and if he were savvy it could contribute to his political rise. He was right. The following year a political ally of Kelly's was elected to the South Park board, and Kelly himself was elected president. Thus the Fine Arts Building was given a reprieve and an opportunity for a new life.

Outside of pure politics, the Fine Arts Building stirred lively debate among architects. One proponent of restoration was George Washington Maher, a well-known Prairie School architect who referred to the building as the "last remaining memorial to a great architectural achievement," by which he meant the World's Columbian Exposition. Maher was no classicist (he eschewed historical precedent in his own work) but was prone to lofty rhetoric. As the campaign to preserve the building heated up, he told a meeting of the Illinois Chapter of the American Institute of Architects that Atwood's design was a thing of genius and would "live as long as art has any appeal to mankind." The chapter formally endorsed restoration.

Not all architects agreed. Their opposition was based on the building's unabashed classicism in an age when modern architecture was bucking hard against the old. Andrew N. Rebori, one of the city's leading modernists, termed the campaign to save the building a "sentimental uprising." The 1920s, he believed, were a time of progressive architecture—of simplicity, practicality and new modes of construction. The Fine Arts Building, on the other hand, "out Greeks the Greeks and does nothing more as far as being of any real potent value to Chicago," Rebori said. He compared Atwood's building to the old Water Tower on Michigan Avenue, which Rebori insisted was nothing but an impediment to traffic.

Other architectural tastemakers opposed renovation on the same grounds. Isaac Pond, of Pond and Pond (architects for much of the Hull House complex for Jane Addams) lambasted the classical design as "a bunch of meretricious detail." Gossip among architects even brought Ernest Graham of Graham, Anderson, Probst and White, the city's leading firm, into the fray. Talk was that Graham opposed the renovation early on, because he feared the restored palace might overshadow the new Field Museum, also classical, which was designed by his firm.

Opposition counted for little against the forces in favor of the restoration. The *Chicago Tribune* was for saving it. Edward J. Kelly was banking his political career on it. In 1922, a federation of South Side women's clubs raised $7,000 to rebuild a section of the northeast corner with concrete and crushed quartz aggregate. This partial restoration was completed to demonstrate how splendid the building could be. It was still unclear what might go inside—a women's memorial hall was another idea. But that decision, said preservationists, would come later. In 1924 the park commissioners asked South Side voters to authorize a $5 million bond issue for a full restoration. The referendum won easily, 49,000 votes to 13,000.

Two years later, when Julius Rosenwald pledged his $3 million for an industrial museum, he put the restoration project on a new and hopefully faster track. With the Rosenwald announcement, Chicago's most important captains of industry were brought into the enterprise. Graham, Anderson, Probst and White was engaged as well to draw up plans for the new museum. If Graham really did wince at Atwood's fine building, the commission for Chicago's largest and most expensive restoration project ever brought him in line with the powerful Commercial Club members who loved it.

INEVITABLY, VISIONS CLASHED WITH REALITY. There were many reasons for delay in getting construction started. Among them was slowness of the architects. "I am quite disgusted with Graham's attitude," Rosenwald wrote in a letter that showed unwonted irritation on his part. "He probably has so much work that he is indifferent. The Opera House has no doubt had first call." Chicago was still, temporarily, in the prosperous Roaring Twenties.

As early as 1928, however, financial problems did present themselves. These problems had more to do with overgreat expectations than profound economic travail, as the Depression was still more than a year away. But bids, when they finally came, were far too high. This situation led to new discussions with the architects, called back to find ways to reduce the cost and stay within the $5 million budget. When Graham's firm took another look at the building, they proposed that cornices and other ornamental detail—cut stone in their original plans—be replaced with terra-cotta. This would save over $300,000.

With a ferocity that took everyone by surprise, the terra-cotta idea caused an uproar. "Words fail me to express my disgust," wrote one taxpayer. He was not alone. Others expressed themselves in favor of hard stone and said that anything less would be regrettable and even disastrous. Costly white marble was the first choice, of course, but in the absence of marble, limestone was essential for a building that was certain to be a major civic monument. The *Chicago Tribune* joined the campaign against terra-cotta—which in turn led to a battery of counterclaims. In an open letter printed on a full page of the *Chicago Tribune*, the Midland Terra Cotta Company declared that their industry was being unjustly slandered on account of the Museum of Science and Industry. "The artists of the Renaissance left such beautiful examples of terra cotta as the Cathedral of Monza, the Certosa near Pavia, and no sculptural work of the great fifteenth century ever surpassed the Singing Gallery done in terra cotta by Luca della Robbia for the Cathedral of Florence in 1430."

Once again, the political winds were unmistakable. South Park Commission president Kelly, in whose hands the decision lay, said that he was "converted by public opinion" to reject terra-cotta for limestone. "A cheaper material is inappropriate for a building intended as a monument of permanent beauty." One of Kelly's commissioners was blunter still: "No woman could be persuaded to accept an imitation pearl if she could afford the genuine."

Affording it, of course, fell to the one man whose pockets were deep and whose reputation seemed to teeter in the balance of this knotty project. In the midst of the terra-cotta quarrel, Julius Rosenwald promised that he would pay for any overrun that reconstruction might bear over the $5 million bond issue. This was in addition to his original promise of $3 million to develop and equip the Museum inside. Through Rosenwald's attorney and Museum board member Leo Wormser, the donor let it be known that the issue of another million dollars "was not nearly as bothersome to the philanthropist as the delay."

Yet another problem to be overcome was an old but persistent one. It was a lawsuit against the South Park Commissioners and the Museum brought by a Chicago lawyer named Thomas Furlong. Furlong's legal battle had begun in 1925, shortly after the commission resolved to spend money on the Fine Arts Building. Representing only himself, Furlong contended that a park district was for parks and had no authority to build or reconstruct buildings. The legal roller coaster took the Furlong case to the state supreme court, which ruled in favor of Furlong, then reversed itself in favor of the commissioners. In 1929, just as the South Park Commission prepared to issue the $5 million in bonds, Furlong renewed his attack, asking for a restraining order against executing the sale.

Furlong's position had little apparent support, certainly not in the press, which observed that this one lawyer was depriving the public of a magnificent new institution. Still, the lawsuit would not go away. In his late attempt to stop the project from starting, Furlong correctly claimed that the original bond issue was passed when commissioners told voters the $5 million was for a new convention center, which was still needed, and now they were getting a museum. The attorney further stated that the commissioners certainly had no right to put the Fine Arts Building in the hands of a private enterprise, which the Museum of Science and Industry was, albeit a nonprofit one. Furlong's final attack came just as construction was scheduled to proceed. It took several more months of frustrating delay before the state supreme court put the issue to rest and this time buried it.

Finally in the fall of 1929—only days before the crash on Wall Street—the reconstruction of the Fine Arts Building commenced. The contractor, R. C. Wieboldt Company (whose bid of $2,649,000 for exterior work was apparently chosen because it was the lowest among the nine submitted), quickly stripped

By 1931, the Museum was taking form in limestone, quarried and cut in Bedford, Indiana. Each detail of the old was reproduced with exactitude in the new—including columns, cornices, caryatids and all other details of the sublime neoclassical exterior.

the building down to bare brick, removing crumbled plaster, gutting the interior and shoring up foundations. Meanwhile the Indiana company chosen to quarry and dress Bedford limestone for the project began its job. This alone would take nine months. The reconstruction of the Fine Arts Building would require more than 53.5 million pounds of limestone, some of which was sculpted into 24 caryatids, each of which was 13 feet tall and weighed six tons. The new building would be essentially an exact replica of the venerable and classical old one.

Little by little, for the next two years, the project took form. The public was impressed. Among letters to editors on the subject, one praised the wonderful classical design of the new museum, but pointed out that in all the hoopla the memory of Charles B. Atwood was being lost. Couldn't he be commemorated with a plaque of some sort? Another somewhat grudging letter came from Irving Pond, the modern architect who had opposed restoration. Admitting that the result was pleasant to look at, Pond tartly recalled that it was sculptor Lorado Taft who deserved credit for the project. Taft's original wish for a museum of sculpture was preempted by other plans, but Pond reminded the public that if they liked the building, they should not lavish too much praise on the politicians.

In fact, the South Park Commissioners did not cover themselves in glory. They themselves were responsible for additional delays. In 1931, the exterior was nearly complete, and workers were ready to begin on the interior when a slight problem arose. The money was not there. This, it was explained, had to do with the Depression. Tax collection was difficult, and the district had trouble making its own ends meet. To solve certain shortfalls, the commissioners chose to borrow from special funds in the commission's control, such as proceeds from the issue of bonds for the Museum. The amount was nearly $1 million, and the commissioners also borrowed special funds set aside for other uses—the completion of Soldier Field was one. Technically, legislation permitted this expedient, but the reputation of Chicago politics was never high, and publicity over this issue was not at all good. Business as usual, the newspapers implied. It also cost the Museum of Science and Industry an additional year in its efforts to open.

The year 1932 came. Museum officials had promised dedication by midyear, but that deadline was now impossible. Then, in the midst of that year of controversy, Julius Rosenwald died after a long battle with heart disease. Rosenwald's death was expected but it caused further uncertainty while his huge estate was settled. Fortunately, the philanthropist's son Lessing was well aware of his father's wish for a museum, and Rosenwald's contributions to the Museum of Science and Industry were assured—and ultimately increased to a total of $7 million. But at that moment, the Museum's future seemed uncertain indeed.

It was fortunate that the public could gaze at the beautiful building rising anew on the edge of Jackson Park, but there was justifiable concern about how long the public's curiosity would last. Finally, the trustees promised a new opening date, June 1933. The Museum of Science and Industry would open alongside another historic spectacle for Chicago, the city's second great world's fair, A Century of Progress.

FIVE

Grand Schemes

There were delays in construction, but the *idea* of the Museum of Science and Industry unfolded with blazing speed. "We shall accomplish in three years what it has taken others twenty-five years to do," said director Waldemar Kaempffert shortly after taking his post in 1928. Success was assured, he said, "because of the wholehearted response of the industries and citizens of Chicago."

Kaempffert's first order of business was to conceive a museum that would mirror his concept of the orderly technological world. He developed an organization of six major divisions, overlapping, to be sure, but each one independent and large enough to fill a significant portion of the Museum. The divisions included Basic Sciences, Mining and Metallurgy, Agriculture and Forestry, Motive Power (such as thermodynamics), Transportation/Communication and Civil Engineering. It was Kaempffert's hope to locate these divisions in some sort of sequence that would demonstrate the logical march of technology through the ages. How this would be done was another question. "Science, engineering and industry are so complex in their interrelationship that it is difficult to grasp the causes and significance of their rapid progress," Kaempffert wrote.

Before leaving on his trip to Europe, Kaempffert hired curators to head each of his six divisions. These were learned young men from colleges and research laboratories, and the director charged them with broad responsibilities to develop exhibits. While Kaempffert was abroad, his staff embarked on traveling of their own. They visited other museums throughout the country. They met with corporations to explain the new Museum and discuss how industry could help. Little by little they determined what was possible—and then some.

On one of these trips, J. A. Folse, curator of motive power, and R. R. Lippold, curator of civil engineering, went east for two weeks with John Maloney, a former reporter for the *New York Times* and the Museum's in-house public relations man. Clearly, some things they saw in established museums did not measure up. The Commercial Museum of Philadelphia, for example, was "one of the most unkempt, unorganized and dirty institutions I have ever seen," Maloney wrote in his report submitted after the trip. The museum was filled with row upon row of so-called historical objects which were often nothing more, he said, than old jugs and bottles. It resembled, Maloney quipped, nothing so much as "an abandoned delicatessen."

More encouraging was a visit to the Newark Museum, founded in 1909 by John Cotton Dana. Dana was well known in the museum world as the apostle of populism. He had written widely on the importance of making museums "speak" to people who visited them. In his book *A Plan for a New Museum*, he wrote, "It is easy for a museum to get objects; it is hard for a museum to get brains." That was one of his pithier remarks, but his whole career was dedicated to celebrating and explaining objects of everyday use.

When the group from Chicago arrived in Newark, they were unable to see Dana, who was by then a very old man. But they did interview his assistant, who gave them a tour. Among many industrial displays, they noticed that the museum print shop was placed in the main hall of the building and was operated as an exhibit. This teaching device, Dana's man admitted, was criticized by eastern connoisseurs as too prosaic for the solemn precincts of a museum. But the people loved it, and so did the visitors from the Museum of Science and Industry.

Other museums on this goodwill tour provided Folse, Lippold and Maloney with additional ideas for exhibits, though one of the most exciting things they saw on their trip was not in a museum at all. It was on the grounds of the Niagara Falls Power Company. In a yard outside a powerhouse and within hearing distance of the roaring water, the company had constructed a scale model of the falls themselves. Some 110 feet by 120 feet, the model had a vertical drop of seven feet.

The visitors from Chicago did not leave Niagara without making copious notes. This was typical of Folse, who began to imagine such an exhibit in Chicago, perhaps containing a model of a hydroelectric turbine. The curator's report on the visit included a full rundown of facts and figures. The power company had paid some $40,000 to construct the miniature falls, he wrote. It could be done in Chicago for a similar amount, unless, of course, a roof was built over it. (It would not fit inside the Museum.) Folse provided further specifications: "The volume of the flow over the model must be 1/12,500 of the volume of flow over Niagara Falls. The latter is normally 210,000 cubic feet per second, so that the flow over the model, to represent normal conditions, should be

16.8 cubic feet per second, or 135 gallons per minute." He added that the cost of pumping water through the model would be 39 cents per hour.

John Maloney's report on the Falls was equally characteristic, in his case that of a salesman selling the attraction to the public. Maloney described the realistic effects of a compressed air unit that made mist around the rush of water. He envisioned illumination at night similar to that at the real Niagara Falls. "I believe the model would attract as much attention as the Buckingham Fountain has done, in addition to being an exhibit of one of the greatest of industries—water power."

Though a model waterfall was never built in Chicago, at the time there was no reason to doubt that it would be done. Indeed, ideas for the new Museum were being generated at an accelerated pace and were taking on a life of their own. News writers faithfully reported what could be expected in the Museum. Academic and professional journals also published articles. In 1929, Russell Anderson, curator of agriculture and forestry, wrote in *Agricultural History* magazine that dioramas and exhibits would illustrate the development of plows and harvesters and would show the full range of farm operations, from irrigation to economic entomology. Here the visitor would see "plant structures and their functions, plant foods and processes, principles and practices of breeding, soils, weather factors, microbiology, etc." Other divisions had equally ambitious plans and wrote about them in detail.

By 1930, so much was going on at the Museum of Science and Industry that an in-house news bulletin was published every two weeks. The news it reported was almost all good:

Item: "The Joseph Dixon Crucible Company has donated an exhibit to the Museum, together with a motion picture film showing how pencils are made." (June 1, 1930)

Item: "Through the assistance of a friend of Mr. Lessing Rosenwald in Pennsylvania the Museum has bought for $75 an old, completely equipped prairie schooner (Conestoga wagon)." (June 15, 1930)

Item: "Sterling Morton, president of the Teletype Corporation, in a recent letter states that 'it is the firm intention of The Teletype Corporation to cooperate with The Museum of Science and Industry in the preparation of a telegraph exhibit.' The Teletype instrument plays an important part in speeding up the relaying of news in the modern newspaper office." (August 1, 1930)

Soon the bulletin announced that donations had reached the 1,000-item mark. This was a positive milestone but not an unmitigated joy. Storage was a problem. Space was rented in various inexpensive warehouses around the city, but the situation reminded Kaempffert of something he had been told by the director of the Techniches Museum in Vienna. It was harder to reject unwanted gifts than to solicit those that were needed.

Other concerns, albeit vague ones, can be found in the pages of the bulletin at that time. Occasionally it noted the activities of the Museum's "competitors." One such item reported that Kaempffert had visited Henry Ford, who was planning an industrial museum in Dearborn, Michigan: "Up to date three million dollars have been spent on his Museum building, and the estimated cost of the completed Museum will be over five million dollars, . . . In accordance with Mr. Ford's policy the Dearborn Museum must pay for itself, but how is not very clear."

AS THE DEPRESSION DEEPENED, financial concerns for the Museum grew, at least among the trustees, who were responsible for paying the bills. Before he died, Julius Rosenwald was one of the first to notice that the Museum's payroll of 70 people seemed large, especially for a museum that was years away from opening. Indeed, expenses were accelerating. In mid-1931, Rosenwald met with board president Rufus Abbott to discuss the situation, and Abbott calculated that the annual operating expenses of the Museum, once open, could be as high as $500,000. Rosenwald noted that his $3 million would not last long without other sources of revenue. He also suggested that Abbott inquire whether members of the Commercial Club would be willing to make cash contributions on a yearly basis. Abbott demurred. Especially in light of the Crash, it was impolitic and probably hopeless to expect each member, well-heeled as most of them were, to contribute $6,000 each year. Yet Abbott offered no alternatives. (He did offer to resign as president around this time.) Financially, the Museum of Science and Industry was headed into uncharted waters.

Less mindful of budgetary constraints were Kaempffert and his curators, whose plans were getting far more publicity than the financial uncertainties were. Kaempffert, to be sure, did not expect to open the Museum with all of his ideas fully realized. He admitted that his detailed outline of each division was only an "ideal plan," and that "no ideal plan can be even remotely realized." Nevertheless, few restraints were placed on the curators as they planned the galleries. Years before the Museum was opened, each division could have filled the entire Museum with exhibits of its own.

It also took time to get the curators to agree on basic goals. At least once, Kaempffert complained that the curators were divided on the real purpose of the institution. One of the curators believed the Museum's role was the "teaching of scientific method." Another one was "strong for vocational guidance." These views were not wholly contradictory. "Let me emphasize once more that ours is an educational institution in the large sense of the term," Kaempffert said. Elementary science could be blended with demonstrations of industry. Whatever the mix, the curators needed to be in concert, and this did not happen immediately.

AS WORK CONTINUED on the Fine Arts Building, Kaempffert was eager to expand his staff—at seeming cross-purposes with the newly budget-minded trustees. By early 1930, Kaempffert envisioned a total of 600 separate exhibits to be ready for the opening of the Museum. To accomplish this he would need a staff of 200—curators, draftsmen, machinists, modelmakers, sculptors and painters. The number of employees in the rented workshops never reached that level, but Kaempffert's operation was a constant wonder to people who saw it, and a significant worry to Museum accountants.

Dioramas of ancient engineering were assembled. Models of locomotives, airplanes and ships were crafted. Machines were devised to demonstrate the principles of magnetism and the refraction of light. In an enthusiastic article, the *Chicago Tribune*'s Lloyd Lewis reported that much work was going on inside the Museum's workshops. "Hundreds of scenic artists and electrical experts are at work all over the country, preparing shadow boxes, perspectives and displays, which are in reality stage effects and will make the educational exhibits dramatic."

The sheer volume of this work and the payroll were difficult for some trustees to swallow. Yet like a director making a feature film, Kaempffert seemed aggressively unaware of fiscal realities. Predictably, problems arose between him and the board, especially President Abbott, who long ago had voiced misgivings about the former newsman's administrative qualifications. There apparently were disagreements between the two, and these led to a showdown. Kaempffert and Abbott left little evidence of their contretemps, as was natural for civilized men at that time. But as small issues grew large, they eventually fueled major conflict.

An early disagreement between Kaempffert and Abbott concerned the election of George Ranney, a director of International Harvester, to the Museum's board of trustees. From Abbott's point of view, Ranney was an excellent choice. His company had history, technology and, above all, clout. For Kaempffert, however, it proved problematic. In a farm equipment exhibit being planned, executives of International Harvester, which was assisting in the display, insisted that their company was the true inventor of the modern farm tractor. Research by Kaempffert and his staff proved otherwise. Kaempffert never forced the issue, and Ranney was welcomed to the board and served for many years. But it highlighted a stark difference in outlook between the scientific executive director and the fiscally minded president.

The final episode between Abbott and Kaempffert took place sometime before Christmas 1930. Construction on the building's exterior was moving along. The trustees, especially Abbott, were keeping a close watch on the details, making certain that every dollar was accounted for. They were distressed that Kaempffert was not doing likewise. Thus Abbott decided to impose additional discipline on administrative matters. He divided the organization into three separate divisions: curatorial, public relations and business. An "assistant director" would take charge of each. These individuals would formally report to Kaempffert, but on many issues assistant directors would deal with the board as well.

The move was unacceptable to Kaempffert, whose anger over what he saw as trustee meddling had been building for some time. Over the holidays he traveled to New York where, unbeknown to the Museum board, he arranged to get his old job back at the *New York Times*. On January 2, Kaempffert resigned from the Museum. When Leo Wormser, who had grown extremely close to Kaempffert, tried to talk him out of the decision, the director said the die was cast. He had promised the *New York Times* that he would be back before spring.

Characteristically, the ailing Julius Rosenwald took the news of Kaempffert's resignation calmly. Also characteristically, he appeared more sympathetic to Rufus Abbott, the realist, and not to Kaempffert, a "dreamer," as he was sometimes described. "A prima donna is difficult to handle," Rosenwald wrote Wormser from a resort in Honolulu. "I am sure Rufus acted wisely and with your concurrence—I was fearful that he would not last—but am sorry for you & the others who are compelled to assume responsibility."

Wormser also regarded the problem as calmly as he could. In a letter to Rosenwald he noted that grand projects such as the Museum were inevitably developed in two separate stages. The first was devising large outlines and schemes as Kaempffert had done. "The second period, as I conceive it, is to project the dreams into reality."

Grand Openings

The Museum of Science and Industry opened to the public on June 19, 1933. There was little fanfare for the event, and great fireworks would have been pointless because the interior was not half finished. Chicago's attention, moreover, was riveted on something else, A Century of Progress, the city's second spectacular world's fair.

Years before, Museum officials had fretted that fair planners would steal their thunder. Now the Museum was happy to have the fair as a neighbor, because A Century of Progress was bringing many millions of people to Chicago, and a good portion of them were sure to visit the Museum as well. Long before either one opened, it was clear that the fair and the Museum shared many common interests.

Aspects of this partnership were formalized. Museum staff agreed to advise fair organizers in the preparation of scientific and industrial exhibits. Museum workshops were also engaged to build dozens of models for the fair's huge Hall of Science. Then, after A Century of Progress closed, these exhibits, and many others from around the world, would go to the Museum. This agreement also provided that one-fourth of all surplus fair profits would go to the Museum—the payment eventually amounted to $40,000. Most important, however, were the intangible benefits of cooperation between A Century of Progress and the Museum of Science and Industry.

For the Museum, those benefits included priceless lessons in striking a balance between education and entertainment. At this, the world's fair's general manager, Lenox R. Lohr, turned out to be a master. To attract visitors, for example, Lohr gave his exposition the look of a carnival, albeit a sophisticated one,

When the Museum opened in 1933, curators emphasized the hands-on approach to science. Pictured here is one of the earliest exhibits, called "Transfer of Momentum," featured in a section devoted to the laws of physics.

with a colorful midway, the Sky Ride hanging 200 feet over a lagoon, and a Ferris wheel. Admission price to the fairgrounds was cheap, averaging less than 50 cents per person, because Lohr believed that large crowds would make exhibitors willing to pay premium prices to be part of it. Moreover, Lohr found that people who got through the gate at nominal cost spent more on guidebooks, rides and countless concessions once they were in.

A Century of Progress was intended as a salute to modern technology, and fair organizers were careful that it should maintain a mostly serious tone. A proposed Heinz 57 pavilion, for example, in the form of a 1,000-ft. pickle, was vetoed by head architect Louis Skidmore. But many parts of Lohr's fair were fanciful, such as the Streets of Paris attraction, with its narrow lanes, make-believe gendarmes and varied exotica. The undisputed star of the Streets of Paris was Sally Rand, whose fan dance seemed to overshadow all the curiosities of science and industry combined. As Rand performed her serpentine act, naked save for two large ostrich-feather fans, she became an instant celebrity. Her act brought massive publicity and thousands of visitors, who only then might wander to the General Motors exhibit or Wonder Bakery.

The fan dance was not the only news being made at the fair. On August 6, 1933, the fan dance shared the front pages with the Piccard stratospheric balloon. The same day that Commander Settle attempted to break the world altitude record from Soldier Field, Chicago's fan dancer made an appearance in Women's Court, having been booked the day before for a dance that some police officers regarded as obscene.

What followed was a full-blown legal circus to decide whether or not the attractive farm girl's dance really was "indecent." The first magistrate before whom Rand appeared, Women's Court Judge Irwin Hasten, appeared liberal on the question. He wondered aloud if the police were not being too hard. "We have progressed," the judge said, "so that now we must distinguish between the beautiful, shapely girl, and the lewd, lascivious burlesque." It was undeniable that Sally Rand had talent with the fans. It was also true, as the *Chicago Daily News* stated, that "the fan dancer was arrested four times yesterday by Policeman Harry Costello and Policewoman Bessie McShane of the morals squad, who maintained . . . that Sally's southern exposure constituted indecency." Fortunately for the newspapers, the case was continued.

By late summer—as the Museum of Science and Industry vied for just a fraction of the attention—Rand was tried in two separate cases. At the first trial, one of the arresting officers took the stand and was asked to describe his feelings as he witnessed the fan dance. "My passions were aroused," he replied evenly. Thus the judge was forced to fine the defendant $25. The legal definition of obscenity was "any action or display which arouses the passions either with or without intent."

At the second trial, the drama played equally well. In this courtroom the prosecutor warned the jury that letting Rand off would "revive the animalism of Greece, approve the lust of Rome, set the stamp of approval on the free love of the middle ages." Here again the presiding judge felt that he was faced with little choice. He convicted her and sentenced her to a year in jail, though it was later reduced to a fine.

ALTHOUGH THE MUSEUM OF SCIENCE AND INDUSTRY was overshadowed by these goings-on, it profited from them as well. Organizers had worked hard to open in time for the crowds that were sure to flock to A Century of Progress. If only a small proportion of them (they numbered 21 million the first year) took the 10-minute bus ride south to the Museum, it would be a great boost. If they were pleased by what they saw and spread the word to others, it could mean a very good start indeed.

To be honest, however, the Museum's first days as a going concern were inauspicious. For several years now, Chicagoans had watched its grand exterior rise. Those who expected something equally lavish inside must have been disappointed; there had been neither time nor money to finish it as hoped by 1933. When the Museum welcomed its first visitors that summer, the floors were raw concrete, and steel reinforcing rods were exposed in many places. Its exhibit area was only as wide as the front doors, large, to be sure, but not what one might have expected or hoped. By fall, a primitive heating system of "salamanders" was installed—metal barrels with smoldering coal inside. Many guides that year complained that the heat seared their clothes if they stood too close— trousers would come back from dry cleaners with creases split from bottom to top.

Happily, many people were enchanted by the new museum just the same. After its soft opening with minimal ceremony, over 300,000 people visited the Museum in its first full year. They saw things they had never seen before. Near the entrance was a full-sized model cow hooked to a modern milking machine. "They've found the ideal cow in Chicago," reported the Associated Press, "one that will supply a steady stream of milk 24 hours a day." To demonstrate the history of printing—one of Chicago's strongest industries—two 19th-century handpresses were in operation. A modern airplane pilot "trainer" attracted young and old alike. Visitors tried to stabilize and steer a suspended model plane through blasts of air by working flaps and rudder with a stick.

The Museum of Science and Industry became known as the "pushbutton museum," making good on Julius Rosenwald's promise that his museum would feature machines in almost endless motion and "no hands-off signs." A "Transfer of Momentum" exhibit unit had a dozen 15-lb. bowling balls strung from wires in a straight line. A visitor could lift the first ball and release it. It would strike the row of eleven, and a single ball would instantly careen in the opposite direction from the other end. Lift two balls, and two would careen. Then three. It was an equal-and-opposite-reaction demonstration—simple but mesmerizing.

There were modern industrial devices in operation, such as the "universal testing machine," which could pull apart thick metal bars, wooden logs and other materials, measuring their strength in small degrees. "The modern hydraulic testing machine measures the load by transmitting it hydraulically through a frictionless, inertialess ram having an almost infinitely small motion in a cylinder to carefully calibrated elastic tube gauges." This description was written by Waldemar Kaempffert in the Museum's first guidebook, *From Cave-Man to Engineer,* which he agreed to prepare after his resignation as executive director. If the words were lost on some visitors, the visual image was not. And a quotation from scientist-philosopher Blaise Pascal clarified the device's importance: "To measure is to economize."

One of the most memorable exhibits of the opening was a demonstration of underwater metal cutting. A demonstrator in a diving suit entered a large windowed tank of water carrying an oxy-electric torch. The torch would make

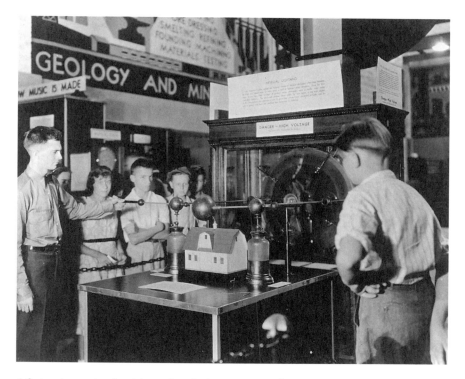

A featured attraction for visitors when the Museum opened was
the electrostatic machine, demonstrating the discharge of lightning in
the atmosphere and how lightning rods were used to protect farm
buildings from destruction in electrical storms.

the water gurgle and boil and, amazingly, it would carve a piece of thick metal
in moments. "The working depth varies from under 80 ft. for river and harbor
work to 200 ft. for deep sea salvage," wrote Kaempffert. "The record is over 300
ft. in salvaging the Submarine F-4 near Honolulu; on the Great Lakes it is 208
ft. at Sturgeon Bay, Wisconsin."

The greatest success of the new Museum of Science and Industry was the
Coal Mine. Almost instantly it became a Museum icon, not only in Chicago but
by reputation all over America. Local papers everywhere picked up articles on
the amazing exhibit. Many visitors to the world's fair were drawn to the Museum
because they had heard of the *Coal Mine*, and when they got there they were
not disappointed. The *Coal Mine* was the work of many people, but much credit
for its success went to Otto T. Kreusser, the director of the Museum who arrived
in 1932.

OTTO KREUSSER WAS HIRED after a search at least as exhaustive as the
one conducted to find Kaempffert. It began with a flurry of newspaper articles

listing the qualifications that such a man should have. Nothing short of a "genius" would do. "He must have the scientific knowledge of an Einstein," Leo Wormser told one reporter, "and the business ability of [General Electric president] Owen Young." These remarks were hyperbolic but expressed a seriousness of mission that the trustees still felt. The "genius" stories also irritated Kaempffert sharply when they reached him in New York. He believed they pointed to his own inadequacies.

Yet the organizers knew that to get the Museum open at all would require someone different from the newspaper man. Kaempffert's successor needed to be more than a philosopher to envision the scope of the great Museum. Rather they needed an organizer who could get results and a "contact man" who could "put across the Museum idea to the captains of industry," as one trustee said.

Over a dozen candidates were seriously considered. Kreusser's name came up when trustee Harold Swift wrote a letter to Charles F. Kettering, the engineering chief of General Motors. Swift did not know Kettering, but they had mutual friends, and Kettering was quick to suggest that his protégé Kreusser might well be the man they were looking for. Kettering was unwilling to let Kreusser, founding director of the General Motors Proving Ground outside Detroit, leave G. M. for good. Any arrangement would be regarded as a "loan," but Kreusser could, if the job were offered, go to Chicago for five years and then return to the company.

Kreusser was a talented man. A New York native, he put himself through Pratt Institute and came out with a degree in automotive engineering. One of his first jobs was on the design of the Liberty Engine, standard equipment in military vehicles in World War I. He later worked for the Dayton Electrical Company, which became the Delco Division of General Motors. Kreusser developed the proving ground where he and his staff diagnosed flaws in pistons, worked on improved suspensions and even invented effective windshield defrosters. If Kreusser was a visionary—and Kettering believed he was—his vision was grounded in the development of real machines for the real marketplace.

Shortly after Wormser traveled to Michigan to meet him, and almost immediately after Kreusser's visit to Chicago, it was decided that this was the man. Kreusser eventually proved that a down-to-earth engineer could also become something of a showman. Although the fabulous *Coal Mine* was not Kreusser's conception, its realization was certainly his. This was only the most conspicuous of his accomplishments in getting the Museum of Science and Industry open.

After assuming his new post in Chicago, Kreusser made several trips to view mining industries throughout the country. He went to the Upper Peninsula of Michigan to visit copper mines. He toured lead mines and even salt mines with the idea that these, too, might be represented in the exhibit space

The *Coal Mine*, one of the earliest and most beloved of all exhibits at the Museum of Science and Industry, was built with a headframe and hoists from a real mine in southern Illinois.

that was waiting on the Museum's ground floor. The mine truly took form when Kreusser found a coal operation in Johnson City, Illinois, which had recently closed because of the Depression. When he saw it, he immediately sought the bankers who owned the headframe, hoists and other equipment that had been repossessed. They were very happy to sell everything to the big, good-natured museum director for the bargain-basement price of $10,000.

This led to the unexpected challenge of getting the pieces of the Museum's largest exhibit to Chicago. Since the headframe could not be broken down into parts, it required an oversized flatbed truck to get it from southern Illinois and maneuver it through Hyde Park to the Museum's doors. This was the first of several logistical operations that would become exhibits of a kind in and of themselves. The next one came two decades later when the U-505 submarine was hauled across Lake Shore Drive.

Once installed, the *Coal Mine* was as realistic as sleight of hand could make it. The miner's elevator ran down a shaft with canvas walls that simultaneously slid upward on rollers. It made the short trip to the basement seem like a long one, hundreds of feet beneath the surface. The miner's train, with a similar "stage curtain," seemed to travel for a mile or more through dark veins of black coal.

Other effects were equally realistic. Workshop personnel were sent to southern Illinois to make plaster casts of a real mine in order to replicate the look and texture of actual veins of coal. More vivid still was something that could not be seen. It was the smell. Kreusser, by working with a perfume manufacturer that took an interest in the problem, came up with a convincing, though expensive, way to achieve the musty, damp odor of a real coal mine.

The illusion was one of a long journey beneath the earth. Over the years it was common for visitors, even adults, to wonder out loud whether the *Coal Mine* was real and whether proceeds from selling coal actually supported the operation of the Museum. Although absolute scientific truth was a firm tenet of the Museum of Science and Industry, demonstrators working in the exhibit were told never to correct visitors who believed they had traveled out beneath the bed of Lake Michigan.

The appeal of the Museum's biggest attraction also owed a debt to the demonstrators hired to work it—they were retired miners from southern Illinois. To city people, these grizzled men were fascinating, with intimate knowledge of pneumatic signals, safety lamps (to prevent ignition of flammable gases) and even the canary cage (where the canary could drop dead of stray methane). They were the Museum's most popular guides, not only because they were the real McCoy but because of their enthusiasm as well. "The miners knew their stuff," remembered Richard Kreusser, son of Otto. "And they were wonderfully enthusiastic. They had no idea that so many people gave a damn about mining."

ALMOST IMMEDIATELY, news of the new museum was widespread. When writers came to Chicago to report on A Century of Progress, they rarely missed

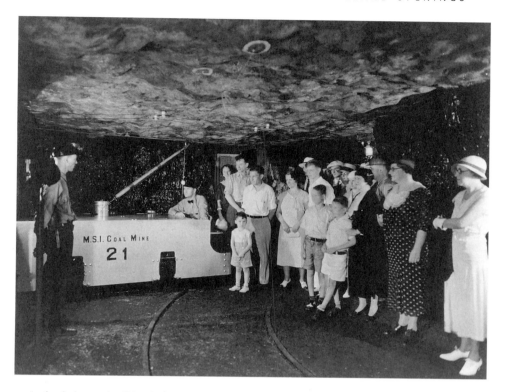

In the dark tunnels of the *Coal Mine*, authentic equipment and experienced miners demonstrated how coal was extracted from the earth to fuel the engine of industrial progress.

the opportunity to see the Museum of Science and Industry. Dignitaries paid their respects as well. When Guglielmo Marconi, inventor of the wireless radio, came from Italy for a visit to Chicago that year, the Museum honored him with a lunch at the Blackstone Hotel. Leo Wormser stated that the trustees were extremely pleased to greet Marconi because the Museum of Science and Industry was dedicated to the great achievements of pioneers like him. "By applying his scientific knowledge to utilitarian purposes he furthered worldly intercommunication and international accord," Wormser said in his address.

This luncheon began a happy relationship between the Museum and the Italian government that lasted for several years. Another visitor to A Century of Progress that year was Italo Balbo, the air force commander who led a mass flight from Rome to Chicago for the fair. Though Balbo was unable to visit the Museum, he promised to donate many valuable models of Italian aircraft that were on display at the fair. These later went into the Museum's first aviation display. For two or three years before World War II (they were removed shortly after Mussolini joined Hitler's axis), Capronis and Savoia Marchettis were well known to many people in Chicago who became familiar with them at the Museum of Science and Industry.

IN 1934, AS A CENTURY OF PROGRESS prepared to close down, the Museum got ready to solicit bids to finish its interior. Unfortunately, financial differences with the park district persisted. At issue was the amount that was left in the bond fund. The Museum claimed that $934,000 remained of the $5 million. The park district claimed that there was only $646,000. A number of factors were responsible for the discrepancy, including the amount of interest accrued when the district borrowed from the Museum bond fund (they claimed they owed no interest at all) and fees assessed by the district (without the Museum's knowledge) for legal and engineering work by park personnel.

Actually, even $900,000 was insufficient to complete the interior of the Museum, and the Rosenwald estate had to make up the difference. Still, the dispute between park commissioners and the Museum led to more delay in construction of the interior, and difficulties deepened in 1934 when Leo Wormser was killed in an automobile accident while vacationing in Michigan. Wormser's skill at negotiating among the scores of people needed to get the Museum this far was indispensable. His absence now was a painful handicap.

Yet plans were too far along—and too many reputations were at stake— for the Museum to be brought to a stop. Already, the architects (now under the name of Shaw, Naess and Murphy after Ernest Graham died in 1935 and left the firm to his successors) had plans for an interior as modern as the machine age itself. The exterior might hark back to classical Greece, but inside would be one of the most distinctive Art Deco interiors of the city. Streamlined design was definitely the fashion of the '30s—functional, smooth, precisely proportioned. Galleries and auditoriums planned for the new interior, stainless steel wainscoting and coved indirect lighting would represent the height of the modern style.

Work to complete the interior was finally set to begin in 1936. (The park commissioners and Museum settled on a figure of $800,000.) It was decided that the project should be completed in two phases: First would come the West Pavilion, the long wing that extended from the central section of the huge building. This would take more than a year to complete, after which the Central Pavilion and its great rotunda beneath the dome could be closed off and finished in turn.

When the West Pavilion was finally finished on March 2, 1938, ceremonies for the dedicatory opening began with a prayer of thanks. "Behold what hath God wrought," the minister said. What he did not need to say was that to get this far, the faith of all concerned was tested aplenty.

This *second* opening of the Museum of Science and Industry featured a cast of characters that showed how much time had passed since the first. Rufus

Dawes, formerly chairman of A Century of Progress, was now president of the Museum. He was a highly respected Chicagoan—brother of the former vice president of the United States—and he brought considerable prestige to the Museum. Dr. Phillip Fox, formerly director of the Adler Planetarium, was now director, having replaced Kreusser, who had been called back to General Motors. Dawes and Fox both prepared remarks for the occasion. Progress was the keynote. Exhibits in the West Pavilion represented progress—the progress of mankind in "the extension and enlargement of knowledge that he might use it for the benefit of human beings," said Dawes.

Edward J. Kelly—former president of the South Park Commission and now Mayor of Chicago—did not attend, but a member of his administration, former alderman Barnet Hodes, spoke for him. Kelly had presided over highs and lows between the trustees and the park district, but on occasions like this there were only the highs. "The great mayor of Chicago" had long harbored faith in the dream of this museum, Hodes said. "The days when Chicago was referred to as the crime capital of the world, the days when Chicago was referred to as the place where the gangster could congregate, those days are gone." Now Chicago could take its place as "a great spiritual and cultural capital of the world."

THE WEST PAVILION had polished galleries and a streamlined 1,000-seat auditorium. It had exhibits about physics and agriculture. There was a hall on automotive engineering which illustrated four-stroke engines and explained antiknock fuel. Most talked about of all was a complete section devoted to the medical sciences. "Too frequently the scientific discoveries that make for the protection of the public health by sanitary engineering measures, vaccination, and serum therapy are neglected by the public," the new guidebook said. A highlight of this gallery was a plastic model of the human body called the *Transparent Anatomical Manikin*. A reporter quipped that this was the rarest of all females—one you could see though—but it was also a highly scientific piece of work. On a pedestal with arms outstretched, the figure showed a skeleton, circulatory system, brain, heart, thyroid and other complex systems visible and realistically portrayed. As buttons were pushed, successive body parts were illuminated by electric bulbs inside.

A year later, one of the most entrancing, and ultimately controversial, exhibits in the Museum was added to the medical science hall. It was a collection of more than 40 fetuses in various stages of development, entitled *Formation of the Human Embryo*. Donated to the Museum by Dr. Helen Button, the specimens were part of her continuing study of obstetrics. Dr. Button began her collection when she was a resident at Cook County Hospital in the early '30s. Cook County was the hospital of the poor, and poverty during the Depression meant that many babies aborted spontaneously because of malnutrition and other problems. Under the circumstances, burial for fetuses often was too costly, so with the permission of the mothers, Dr. Button preserved them in formaldehyde.

The specimens were first placed on public view at A Century of Progress. The collection drew much attention at the fair, and this prompted Dr. Button subsequently to give the collection to the Museum. From the time it was installed there in 1939, the embryo exhibit was one area where the usual background noise of the Museum subsided. "I always found that it was a place where mothers and children talked quietly," remembered Dr. Button.

Although the embryo exhibit has always drawn much attention (singer Michael Jackson once declared that it was his favorite exhibit in the Museum), it avoided controversy for more than 50 years. Then in the late 1980s, with the abortion issue raging, the scientific specimens became a predictable lightning rod. For years, a label beside the exhibit credited Loyola University Medical School, Dr. Button's alma mater, as the source of the collection. Some Loyola physicians reported getting harsh mail from antiabortion advocates who assumed these were the result of intentional abortions. The potential for trouble motivated the Museum to reinstall and reinterpret the exhibit with the new title *Prenatal Development* in 1991. New descriptive labels emphasized that the fetuses did not die because of medical abortions. "Their survival was prevented by natural causes or accidents," a label stated.

Medical exhibits often generate strong reactions. Also installed in the late '30s was *Anatomical Sections*, otherwise known as Body Slices. Preserved and framed in solution, these full-size, inch-thick sections were from cadavers frozen solid to facilitate cutting. Four vertical sections of a female from head to pelvis show relative positions of brain, and thoracic and abdominal organs. Horizontal sections of a male depict slices of head, neck and other parts down to thighs, leg and foot.

These rare specimens remain one of the more popular, if slightly ghoulish, exhibits of the Museum. Body Slices has also led to "urban legends" or rumors connected to the Museum. One legend is that the two individuals in the exhibit were a married couple. They wished to give their bodies to science but also remain united in death. There is no evidence that this is true, and it probably is not.

IF STRANGE AND PECULIAR SIGHTS drew some visitors to the Museum, it was certain that the domed Central Pavilion, when completed, would be a great attraction as well. Immediately after the opening of the West Pavilion, this work began, and anticipation mounted for yet another opening. Among the finishing touches was a gold-lettered inscription that circled the base of the dome: "Science discerns the laws of nature. Industry applies them to the needs of man." It was an original quotation composed by the curators.

Also a matter of pride were bronze reliefs cast for the main doors of the Museum and the entrance vestibule. Fourteen different panels were symbolic of the many branches of science and technology. One panel for mathematics depicted a logarithmic spiral and Pythagorean construction with "God always geometrizes" written in Greek underneath. In the stainless steel vestibule, plaques honored Zeus, Prometheus and other gods who signified the mysteries of the universe.

Other attractions got much publicity as well. The *Foucault Pendulum*, like the one in the Pantheon of Paris, with a 350-lb. brass orb on a 65-ft. wire, would hang in the three-story west stairwell over a compass of 360 degrees. Originally invented by French physicist Jean Foucault in the 19th century, it demonstrated that the earth does in fact rotate while a pendulum moves in an unchanging plane. The *Foucault Pendulum* was also a handsome piece of art.

Even as press photographers were allowed in to shoot the rapidly filling galleries—of locomotives and antique aircraft in the Hall of Transportation—there were more delays. By the beginning of 1940, with uncertainties looming over the war in Europe, the main doors remained closed. Visitors could wander into new sections as they were completed, but much of the Museum still had the look and feel of an unfinished work. Companies that had donated exhibits began to grumble. Where were theirs? Restless trustees were becoming irritated.

Seven years after its original opening, the Museum of Science and Industry crawled toward completion. It was not just delays that were a matter of concern, however. It was finances. Although the people of Chicago seemed pleased, even dazzled, by each new exhibit that opened, the men ultimately responsible for the Museum were asking a more serious question. Would they have the money to survive for more than a few short years?

Lenox Lohr, himself an avid auto collector, made the Museum one of the
Midwest's most important meccas for antique and classic cars. Here, the
"Major" takes a 1911 Buick around the parking lot for a spin.

SEVEN

The Coming of Major Lohr

Most of the news written about the Museum of Science and Industry had been very good, but there were times when the press wondered out loud about the Museum's future. The Museum sometimes seemed out of focus.

"Opinions Vary on Simplifying Museum Name" was a headline in 1935. Many people in Chicago, the article noted, were calling it the "Science Museum." Others interviewed thought the word "museum" should be eliminated altogether, because it implied a place primarily for old things. Ultimately, "The Museum of Science and Industry Founded by Julius Rosenwald" was not changed, but the issue itself revealed a measure of confusion over what the place was and what it should become.

Within the Museum, director Phillip Fox and his staff were confident that their work was of true scientific merit. Indeed, many highlights in the West Pavilion drew healthy crowds, such as devices generating electromagnetism and a whole room designed to demonstrate the reflection of sound, called the *Whispering Gallery*. What was missing, however, was industry, and the Museum needed not just industry's story but also its financial support. Operating deficits were mounting.

Board president Rufus Dawes, former chairman of A Century of Progress, was particularly distressed by the Museum's direction. He was by now an old man, discouraged by his failing eyesight and by fear of failure in this, his final civic project. The institution was not broke. There was sufficient money to finish the interior, and the treasury would be able to keep the institution running for a few years. But it was painfully clear that the current situation could not continue.

Specifically, operating expenses in the late '30s were in

excess of $400,000 annually. Revenues were less than $100,000, including dividends on 25,000 shares of Sears, Roebuck & Company stock paying $3 per share per year, and *Coal Mine* admissions, which were $20,000 at 25 cents per person. At this rate, the Museum would soon spend its way into oblivion.

The idea of selling tickets at the door was rejected at the time. General admission remained free, which was the preference of Rosenwald and the founders, and state law governing museums on park land in that period required two days per week of free admission anyway. Other moneymaking schemes were attempted (with an eye on the popularity of the *Coal Mine*). A "liquid air" demonstration was set up with a small admission charge, but it was unsuccessful, and the failure turned to tragedy when a demonstrator was killed by an explosion from an oxygen tank.

Toward the end of 1939, a despondent Rufus Dawes looked forward to the visit of Major Lenox Lohr to Chicago. Lohr, then 48, had been general manager of A Century of Progress and was regarded as a primary reason for its success. He was now president of the National Broadcasting Company. Dawes and Lohr were close—it was a kind of father-son relationship—and Lohr was alarmed when Dawes darkly asked that they meet in complete privacy. Then when they were together in Lohr's hotel room, the older man explained that the Museum of Science and Industry was in a desperate situation. The Museum was hemorrhaging money, its curators were at odds with one another, and Dawes was getting conflicting reports from them. Because of his near blindness, he felt helpless to sort the situation out.

While Lohr was a trustee of the Museum, elected after the fair, his duties at NBC made it impossible for him to be closely involved. The meeting with Dawes left him with sharp pangs of regret, and the Museum was much on his mind when he took the train back to New York.

Early the next month, Lohr received word that Dawes had died of a heart attack. It saddened Lohr deeply, especially that the career of his good friend should end on such a note. Yet Lohr had difficulties of his own at that time— he was coping with the hardships of working for General David Sarnoff, the first of a long line of high-pressure executives to run the broadcast industry.

A few months later, Chicago banker Philip R. Clarke, a new trustee of the Museum, was in New York for a board meeting of the United States Steel Corporation. As Clarke later recounted, he was on his way to Pennsylvania Station to catch the train back home when he ran into Lohr on the street. Their conversation outside the station was cordial and brief. They exchanged remarks about Rufus Dawes. Lohr said he would like to do something to help the Museum, if only for the sake of his late mentor.

With this conversation in mind, Clarke called Lohr's office as soon as he returned to Chicago. He asked for an appointment the following week, as the banker was planning another trip to New York. When he visited Lohr at his NBC office, he outlined what the Museum of Science and Industry needed in a new president, and he asked Lohr what he thought. For an hour or so they discussed the problem in general terms, and then Clarke left. Several weeks later they met in New York again, and Lohr recommended several candidates for a full-time president, which the trustees agreed was needed. Lohr listed their qualifications and described how they might be approached.

At a certain point in this meeting, "I decided it was time to strike," Clarke later said. He told Lohr that Lohr himself was the best man for the position. He was an engineer, adept at management and certainly had the spark of a showman. Clarke was adamant, saying that Lohr "would leave his footprints more indelibly in the sands of time as president of the Museum of Science and Industry than a hundred presidents of the National Broadcasting Company."

It took several weeks to decide, but Lohr eventually came to the same conclusion. By June 1940, he resigned his job at NBC and became the full-time president of the Museum at a salary of $25,000. (He had been making $60,000 at NBC.) "The Major," as he was called by all who knew him, arrived in Chicago a few months before the formal opening of the Museum's Central Pavilion. As he got ready to assume the post, he had no trouble attracting attention. He sat for numerous interviews, telling reporters that he shared the late Julius Rosenwald's image of the Museum as a place of excitement. "I visualize the institution," Lohr told the *Chicago Tribune*, "as a great national museum, a show, in which science and industry will live as dramatic things."

Getting to that point might take time, of course. When Lohr got to Chicago he created some instant drama of another kind. He fired Phillip Fox, the director, most of the ranking curators and an assortment of other employees. Dr. Fox's first intimation of trouble came the day before Lohr's formal election by the board. He received a letter from F. C. Boggs, a longtime Museum trustee and a good friend of Lohr's from the fair days. Boggs informed Fox that Lohr intended to combine the duties of president and director: "I am sure he will take over practically all the work you have been doing." Fox would do well to resign immediately. A few days later, 13 salaried employees were summarily dismissed, most of them even before meeting the new president. A number of hourly personnel also went. Lohr's purge, done in the name of financial necessity, marked a new chapter in the Museum's management. The Major was only getting started

Unexpectedly, Fox did not take the action lying down. In a letter to the trustees of the Museum—some of whom had no advance knowledge of the firings—he appealed for reversal. The "Fighting Star Gazer" (Fox was an astronomer who had had a distinguished military career) insisted that preparation of exhibits was proceeding with all due speed and according to plan.

"Throughout the whole Museum, in every hall, the plan is revealed in clear-cut exhibits of meticulous scientific accuracy," he wrote. He claimed that the Museum's finances were not untenable, and in any case, he had reviewed all expenditures with the late Mr. Dawes.

Fox's long letter went on in often inflammatory terms. But his effort was for naught. The board did not reverse his "resignation," whereupon Fox submitted the letter to *Science* magazine. In doing so he made the issue a public debate, framed as business versus scholarship. "It is an affront to the intelligence of the community," Fox wrote. "It has started unfavorable comment in the scientific world; it has been termed a 'blitzkrieg' and 'Nazism' in the public press."

Lohr and the board held fast, but the storm did not subside as quickly as they hoped. Local members of the scientific community entered the fray. At the University of Chicago, which maintained scholarly relations with the Museum, an ad hoc committee was quickly formed to look into the situation. They produced a report that stated that there was "no evidence that the board of trustees consulted competent men, outside its own ranks and the Museum staff, in reaching a decision." It was "contrary to justice." Nobel Prize winner Arthur H. Compton, a member of the committee, also spoke to local newspapers. "A tragedy has occurred in the cultural life of our city," he told the *Chicago Daily News*. To a *Chicago Herald-American* reporter he said, "Financial problems cannot justify a diversion of the museum from its proper aim."

Lohr did not respond. Nor did he bend when personal letters of appeal came, including one from a priest written on behalf of a fired shop worker. The Major's steadfast attitude in this squared with his military background. It was a quality that the trustees appreciated under the circumstances.

LENOX LOHR WAS INDEED A MILITARY MAN at heart, and remained so throughout his 28-year career at the Museum. He was a 1916 graduate of Cornell University. With a degree in mechanical engineering, he joined the Army and was quickly commissioned as a second lieutenant in the Corps of Engineers. Serving in France during World War I, he received the Silver Star for gallantry in the Meuse-Argonne offensive. Later he became executive secretary of the Society of American Military Engineers and editor of its journal, *Military Engineer*, rising in this process to the rank of major.

In these Washington-based posts, Lohr came to the attention of Coolidge's vice president, Charles Dawes, and his brother Rufus Dawes. They admired Lohr's business mind-set combined with military discipline. Then, in 1932, Lohr was due for promotion within the Army, but the new assignment that loomed involved a transfer to Alaska. He therefore accepted the Daweses' offer to become general manager of A Century of Progress, where he flourished for the fair's two-year run. His success in Chicago had much to do with his being offered the presidency of NBC.

WHILE AVOIDING A PUBLIC DEBATE over the Museum firings, Lohr still engaged the press and provided them with provocative material. To one writer he admitted that he wasn't sure he liked the word "museum." Without promising to change it, he said "theater" was more to his liking. "While we have valuable things, our chief objective is to prove that science is a living thing," he said. Lohr also declared that the dreary color scheme of the exhibits would be enlivened, recalling that the fair of 1933 was one of the most colorful events ever. In general, the needs of the average visitor would come first. Labels on exhibits were going to be rewritten in plainer English. To top it off, smoking would be permitted in the building. The public had reason to be curious.

And employees who remained had reason to be encouraged. One of the Major's first actions as president was to conduct regular meetings with the staff—not mandatory, but optional, as an opportunity to discuss the management of the place. Lohr held forth at these meetings and expounded on many of his ideas. At one, he explained that the role of the Museum was "informal education," which differed entirely, he insisted, from "formal education." Formal education was sequential, regimented and required attendance. Informal education was noncompulsory, so it needed to be enjoyable. It was therefore the responsibility of absolutely everyone working at the Museum of Science and Industry to make every visitor's experience positive. Each employee, from the Major on down, was an ambassador of goodwill and a "continuous salesman for the museum." It was with this in mind that guides and demonstrators working in exhibit areas were put in uniform.

The Lohr regime began well despite the initial shock. Esprit de corps was quickly raised. Suggestions began coming in from the troops, and some of them wrote thoughtful letters to the new president. One of these emphasized the need to explain the deeper meaning behind the machines in the exhibits. "I like your way of showing that the machine age contributed material wealth to our nation, contrasted with the taboo idea that mass production is responsible for our political ills," wrote an exhibit demonstrator named Sam Rosenthal.

If there appeared to be a measure of employee participation at the Museum, there was still no doubt about who was in charge. With military precision, the Museum day began at 9:30 sharp. (Lohr himself was a late riser and sometimes got to work from his home in Evanston as late as 10:30 a.m.) Duplicate memorandums were de rigueur. To oversee all such details, Lohr hired a trusted assistant as a sort of lieutenant. Martha McGrew had worked for the major at A Century of Progress. She had moved to New York to work for him at NBC. At the Museum she engendered a certain amount of fear. "Miss McGrew knew absolutely everything that was going on," said one young employee from that period. She was an ageless spinster and wore a hearing aid that worked well when she needed information but malfunctioned frequently when she was asked for some special dispensation.

While Miss McGrew kept the staff on its toes, Major Lohr could wander the halls of the Museum in his avuncular way. He would talk to demonstrators, suggest small improvements, but mostly collect impressions and form ideas. Then he would go back to his office—which he located directly next to the front entrance—close the door, and dictate into his tape recorder. In these tapes, especially the early ones, Lohr reflected on what he needed to do to succeed in his new job. Among his earliest observations was that the Museum must solicit and secure substantial industry support. And that support would come only if the Museum became a place to tell the story of corporate America. Lohr said that big business was widely distrusted at this time partly because it rarely engaged in public dialogue. "It is our purpose to solicit the cooperation of the companies forming these industries," he said. "We will afford them a great opportunity not only for public service but for material reward." Corporate sponsorship would be the Museum's way out of financial trouble.

But, Lohr warned, exhibits were not a place for advertising. His ideal museum, revealed in these tapes, was an embassy of ideas. Education, and not trade, was its mission. The balancing act between promotion and philanthropy would require subtlety on the part of companies—because it was the companies themselves that would tell their own stories with their own experts. But the result would be in everyone's interest. A visitor would feel no need to "build up sales resistance against the product, as he knows that no selling will be attempted. He is, therefore, in a most receptive state of mind to absorb the merits of a product or process."

In other tapes, Lohr mused on history's geniuses. He talked about the "age-old desire to find the truth"—from Leonardo da Vinci to Heinrich Hertz, who studied electromagnetism, to Bell, Marconi and the Wright brothers. He cautioned, however, that the Museum was primarily a place for the *recent* episodes of technology. The amazing inventions of the present day were what the public wanted to see, and equally important, they were what sponsors wanted to exhibit. Lohr believed absolutely that he could funnel the commercial needs of companies into a true educational role for the public. Competitive product claims were verboten. Scientific principles would rise to the surface. Lohr was certain that his objectives would be broad enough for all to embrace.

"The Museum offers a medium through which Industry can combat the antagonism toward capitalistic structures," he said. "If it can promote a friendlier spirit and better understanding between capital and labor, between producer and consumer . . . then I think the Museum will have done all that its founder, Julius Rosenwald, hoped it would do."

IN THE EARLY AFTERNOON OF JANUARY 29, 1941, people throughout the country turned on their radio sets and listened in on a scene set in Pennsylvania in 1829. A man named Horatio Allen was testing the very first locomotive in the United States, an English import called the *Stourbridge Lion*.

It was a tense moment as Allen stoked the boiler and readied to go. He knew that the rails built for the occasion were weak, and the trestle across a small river was untested for this three-and-a-half-ton engine. Allen ordered all onlookers off his train. "One man's life is enough to risk with all that's at stake here today," he cried.

This quaint script was performed from the Museum of Science and Industry over the entire NBC radio network. As a light historical drama, it was a moment of relief for listeners who were getting increasing war news from Europe. The Battle of Britain had just ended. Hitler's buzz bombs continued to terrorize London. The American public was hearing this bad news often in live broadcasts from pioneer correspondents such as Edward R. Murrow, reporting from rooftops amid explosions. Here, instead, was history of a gentler kind, but not without theatricality all its own.

Horatio Allen began moving the *Lion* over the makeshift track. Men shouted. Women screamed, and the timbers holding the trestle creaked. But the engine made it across, and the crowd was jubilant. As the program continued, listeners who tuned in late found out why the story of railroading was being told. The occasion was the formal opening of the newly renovated Central Pavilion and the introduction of a new exhibit, the largest miniature railroad in the world. On hand were over 500 dignitaries, including the board of directors of the Atchison, Topeka and Santa Fe Railroad, the exhibit's sponsor. Once Horatio Allen was safe and the luncheon was cleared away, opera star Vivian della Chiesa entertained with Rossini's "Tarantella." Then Edward Engel, president of Santa Fe, and Major Lohr made short speeches.

Receptions and celebrations honoring sponsors became typical of the Lohr regime, and this was Santa Fe's day. Indeed, the model railroad was one of the most impressive exhibits ever in the Museum. The creation of legendary model railroader Minton Cronkhite, it was built to Cronkhite's own "Q gauge," similar to "O" but considered more realistic in scale. Four full-length trains traveled on 1,000 feet of track through 40 switches, with a signal system of red, yellow and green lights duplicating the system on the actual railroad. It was a 3,000 sq. ft. microcosm of America, with mountains, tunnels, forests, cotton fields, mines and even a section of the Grand Canyon. On the miniature landscape, an oil refinery, a cement plant and other industrial sites that even included a rail car repair shop featured intricate moving parts (such as miniature lathes and a boring mill).

The Museum & Santa Fe Railroad, as it was called, became the centerpiece of the Hall of Transportation, with antique engines such as the Mississippi, built in 1834 and the oldest existing locomotive from the South, and the Pioneer, built in 1848, the first ever run from Chicago. Above were biplanes and other vintage aircraft hung from the ceiling on cables. Although these pieces were motionless, the model railroad seemed to animate the whole room.

When Santa Fe's Engel got up to speak at the broadcast event, he briefly

The Museum & Santa Fe Railroad was unveiled in 1941. Designed and built by famed model builder Minton Cronkhite of California, it was once regarded as the largest and most authentic miniature railroad in the world. Pictured here not long after its opening, *The Museum & Santa Fe* showed how railroads provided essential links between the nation's varied landscapes and many different industries.

described the growth of the railroad. He recalled the days of slow transportation and asked the audience to appreciate the improvements in life that were the result of the modern railroad. "Thirty thousand trains are operated daily in the United States and this mass transportation continues night and day in fair weather or foul." It was the tenor of the times and of this occasion that a measure of patriotism was in place as well. America was drawing close to war. "Whatever may be the result of the present worldwide disturbance," said Engel, "the railroads look forward with confidence and courage and with determination to perform creditably for the good of the nation and the world the important duties which will be theirs in the great undertaking in which we are now engaged."

When Lenox Lohr rose to accept the Santa Fe exhibit, he agreed that "in these days of strife and uncertainty our American way of life is under constant discussion. We are called upon for an 'all out' effort in its defense." With that in mind, this model railroad "vividly demonstrates the Museum's theme—the partnership of science and industry."

Forgotten, perhaps, was the fact that Phillip Fox and Rufus Dawes had actually initiated this happy relationship with Santa Fe. But the event was a long-awaited triumph for the Museum of Science and Industry. To Lenox Lohr went credit for a media event that made other sponsors hungry to open an exhibit at the South Side museum as well.

Once a part of the World's Columbian Exposition, the building housing the Museum of Science and Industry was the last vestige of the great White City. In the 1930s and 40s, it became the nation's model of an American technological museum.

The Museum Comes of Age

If the mission of the Museum of Science and Industry remained fuzzy in the 1930s, it took form with crystal clarity in the '40s. Lenox Lohr was the most obvious reason for the transformation. Though he was a salesman by disposition and not an educator, the Major had no tolerance for ambiguity, in the organization of his staff or the content of his exhibits.

Lohr's ambitious plans for the Museum naturally caused concern about an unholy alliance between commerce and education, with many of these misgivings coming from the Museum's close neighbor, the University of Chicago. Already Lohr had incurred the wrath of one of the university's Nobel laureates, Arthur H. Compton, who had strongly condemned the firing of Fox. Yet Lohr, who was busy designing an alliance with private corporations, was equally determined to reestablish one with the university.

In his first months at the Museum, Lohr wrote a series of letters to Robert Maynard Hutchins, president of the University of Chicago, inquiring if the relationship between the two institutions could be revived. Hutchins did not respond at first. He, too, was furious about Lohr's handling of the curator situation. Another blow against scholarship, Hutchins believed, and higher education was under ample criticism already.

Nevertheless, there was a kindred spirit between Lohr, the avowed showman, and Hutchins, the intellectual. Both were convinced that the public possessed untapped curiosity and intelligence. For his part, Hutchins deplored the idea that most Americans regarded education like measles or the mumps. "Having had education once," he deadpanned, "you need not, indeed can not, have it again. You put it behind you with your other juvenile troubles." A true believer in lifelong education, Hutchins recognized the potential of the Museum of Science and Industry, despite the recent past. Ultimately he agreed to meet with Lohr. Lohr said the Museum needed the university's help in making exhibits scientifically correct. Hutchins, still a bit cool, said it could be arranged.

A "cooperative plan" was drawn up between the two institutions, and almost immediately more than a dozen members of the university's physics, chemistry and education departments became involved, some of them enthusiastically. A few of these relationships grew into true partnerships. University of Chicago physics professor Dr. Harvey Lemon, a noted author of science textbooks, took a leave of absence from the university in 1941 to become Lohr's curator of physical sciences, and eventually the Museum's scientific director. Others from the university found the huge museum irresistible and used it as a resource for their own studies. Among them was a young student named Lucy Nielsen. Nielsen, working on a Ph.D. in education, was at the Museum less than three years, but in that time her research broke important new ground in the design and function of exhibits to teach science.

Lucy Nielsen had long been enchanted by the Museum of Science and Industry. She had been a precocious science student ever since her father, an engineer, took her to visit A Century of Progress when she was a little girl. At the age of 14, she was admitted to the University of Chicago, where she initially planned to prepare for medical school. Her first years in college, Nielsen later admitted, were not an easy ride. She was discouraged from becoming a physician because she was a woman. She eventually majored in physics, but her talent as a violinist was another impediment to her studies, for she also belonged to several music organizations and scheduled herself to play concerts almost every weekend. As she matured, however, and focused her attention, Nielsen's achievements were substantial. At the age of 19, she graduated from college and started on her graduate degree. Shortly thereafter she was made associate curator of physics at the Museum. Perhaps more than anyone else in the early 1940s, it was she who discovered what museums could accomplish in the field of science education.

Lucy Nielsen had not set out to reinvent American museums. In 1941, she was simply looking for a job to fill the summer before her senior year in college. Because she lived in Hyde Park, it was only natural for her to apply at the Museum of Science and Industry, where she might use her knowledge of astronomy, sound, electromagnetism and other subjects that she had learned as an undergraduate. For its part, the Museum was short of labor because of the war, and Lucy was quickly hired as a demonstrator.

Her first job was to give short lectures to visitors in the physical science hall and operate the exhibits, such as the Van de Graaff generator, which collected and transferred static electricity, and the Tesla Coil, transformer of alternating current into high-frequency electricity for X-rays. She enjoyed it greatly but had not been there long before she realized that something was wrong at the Museum. The labels that accompanied the scientific exhibits were completely baffling. "It was as if they were written by people whose intention was to impress and confuse the public," she said. This was a severe condemnation of the Museum's old regime but squared with the views of Lohr, Lemon and others, who were well aware of the Museum's need for greater simplicity.

When Nielsen got her bachelor's degree the next year, her experience at the Museum helped her decide what to do next. She now knew she had a knack for education, and the challenge of making complicated subjects clear gave her joy. She enrolled in the university's school of education. Perhaps she would be a teacher. But the graduate program at Chicago was highly theoretical. Its research revolved around a subject that had already intrigued Nielsen: how people learn.

Besides her studies, Nielsen took on additional duties at the Museum, filling in for Harvey Lemon who had left for wartime service at the Aberdeen Proving Ground in Maryland, where he was involved in ordnance and weapons testing. This gave the young woman what amounted to two full-time jobs, school and the Museum, a heavy load but tied together in an interesting way. For the next several years, her life was focused on reading about techniques for teaching science and applying them in the nation's largest museum of technology.

At school, Nielsen read everything she could on the subject. At the Museum, she began by rewriting labels, deleting impossible paragraphs on Newtonian mechanics, shortening and simplifying. In the old "Transfer of Momentum" exhibit—the one with 12 swinging bowling balls—she explained the principle involved in terms she believed everyone could understand. Momentum, she wrote, is the product of velocity and mass. It is the reason why a slow moving car is as dangerous to human safety as a speeding bullet.

Until this time, the educational potential of American museums had been widely discussed, but in reality it was little more than the fond hope of many curators. Nielsen was quick to recognize the problem: no one had systematically analyzed an average visitor's ability to absorb technical ideas. In the years that followed, Nielsen did steady research into the problem. "In reviewing the progress thus far made by museums towards attaining their goal of becoming a vital force in broadening the experience and understanding of the citizens of our democracy," she wrote in one of her many papers, "one cannot refrain from asking why this important movement has been so slow in gaining momentum." She concluded that museums simply had "not yet succeeded in establishing for themselves a recognized place in the educational sun."

Nielsen's objective became no less than an attempt to change the status quo. With the Museum of Science and Industry as a huge laboratory, she would succeed in discovering new ways to make the American museum an effective tool in science education.

MAJOR LOHR WAS ALSO WONDERING how to reach the public, although he saw the problem in different terms. He was concerned with World War II. When Lohr arrived at the Museum in 1940, the war was inevitable, and his plan for corporate sponsorships had to be put on hold. At the same time, Lohr knew that nothing held the public's attention like a true national emergency, and this one was to touch the lives of all Americans. The result was that shortly after the United States entered the war, the Museum of Science and Industry carved out an essential home-front role for itself. Not unexpectedly, that role also met Lohr's need to make his museum a popular success.

As the Museum improved old exhibits and developed new ones, many exhibits had a clear military or wartime focus. In numerous ways, the war provided an answer to the one question that all educators face: Do these lessons really matter? Industry was gearing up for combat. American men were embarking for battles the world over. The answer was yes—science and technology obviously mattered very much indeed.

In a pamphlet called *The Museum Goes to War*, Lohr outlined the importance of the Museum of Science and Industry: "Machine tools, metal working, petroleum, coal, steel, agriculture—these are among the important things in a nation at war." The Museum was also involved in a wide range of training. Shortly after Pearl Harbor, the Museum developed technical programs for several organizations that were part of the great national emergency. Among these was the American Red Cross Women's Motor Corps, which was entrusted with much stateside transportation of people and equipment for the duration of the war. A critical issue for the Motor Corps was that few women were familiar with automobile mechanics—breakdowns and delays were a constant risk.

To help solve this problem, Lohr and his staff devised a course at the Museum to familiarize the corps with basic repairs and other situations connected to driving. "As a Red Cross Driver," wrote James Van Pelt in the course manual, "much will depend upon the condition of your car, your skill in driving it, your ability to make emergency repairs." Knowledge of universal joints and shock absorbers and hints on how to conserve precious wartime rubber in tires were among the many lessons that corps women were taught.

Women on the home front were also the focus of a new exhibit in 1942: *The Homemaker and the War*. Its purpose was to explain how housewives could perform their duties efficiently during a time of war. Amid a number of modern appliances (made available by sponsor Westinghouse Electric), this exhibit explained the importance of the rationing of food, the preservation of cooking oils and even the saving of a portion of the household budget to purchase bonds. A home economist was on the premises to answer questions, and motion pictures were shown on the care and use of the stoves, washers and other household appliances, hard to repair in the wartime economy.

Another family-oriented exhibit during the war years was *Civilian Defense*.

The Museum of Science and Industry performed a role during World
War II in training soldiers and teaching important lessons to the civilian
population. An exhibit entitled *The Homemaker and the War* demonstrated
how efficient meal preparation on the homefront aided the military
effort overseas.

Preparation for the possibility of attack was a nationwide concern. Former
mayor Edward J. Kelly was the local coordinator of the Office of Civilian
Defense, and a large portion of the West Pavilion was devoted to the exhibit.
With photo murals, dioramas and a variety of interactive devices, it reviewed air
raid shelters, emergency transportation and medical facilities that would be
used in the event of attack. One diorama, "Blackout Aerorama," provided a
pilot's-eye view of the Chicago area—buildings, bridges and the rural areas
around it. As visitors pushed buttons, the scene went from daytime to night-

time, then nighttime under blackout conditions. The point was to illustrate the importance of turning off lights if an air raid signal were sounded for an enemy attack. The *Civilian Defense* exhibit was extremely popular and also a milestone in the evolution of the Museum of Science and Industry. It was a near-perfect combination of an urgent message and interactive media to communicate it.

World War II was only too real to many Chicagoans at the time, but the Museum played a role in making it more vivid than ever before. The Museum's blockbuster of 1943 was *British War Relics*, an exhibit with authentic war material that most Americans had never seen. Aircraft were always a big attraction at the Museum, and among the artifacts sent by the British Information Service was a German Stuka, a dive-bomber of the type that terrorized Poland and France early in the war. The plane, painted in full camouflage colors, was captured by British forces in North Africa.

British War Relics was not highly technical, but it had high emotional content. This was quite the point. "Never before has there been such an example of cooperation and integration in the work of the military forces of two great nations," said British Consul General W. H. Gallienne at the opening of the exhibit in November 1943, just as Berlin was beginning to bow under the force of allied bombs.

True to form, Lohr used the exhibit for maximum publicity for the Museum as well. Shortly after opening *British War Relics*, he arranged for a British flyer accompanying the exhibit, Lieutenant Wyndam Webber, to be heard on a local radio show called *For Women Only*. Before the war, Webber explained, he had been a sheep farmer "living a peaceful life on England's green pasture lands." But that changed when the Germans began spoiling all that was lovely in his country. Webber, like all his countrymen, was only too glad to give Jerry what he had coming.

Radio had an important, even comforting role on the home front during the war. Since *For Women Only* was a family program, the host asked Webber to explain a pilot's haberdashery. Indeed, a pilot's uniform was substantial, he replied. Keeping warm thousands of feet above ground required many layers of silk, wool and leather clothing. Also on the radio that morning was Army WAC Sergeant Margaret Stanley, who admitted that her uniform was simple by comparison. Yet "the minute you become a WAC, you stop being an individual. It's not because of personal pride alone that you shine your insignia and press your uniform," she said. "You're proud of the Army. You see, it goes far deeper than mere feminine vanity." Most people believed this pleasant banter aided morale. It certainly brought more visitors to the Museum.

LUCY NIELSEN'S WARTIME SERVICE also occurred at the Museum—lecturing to some of the hundreds of military recruits who passed through the Museum as part of their training. Men from the Navy Aviation Machinists School and midshipmen from Abbott Hall at Northwestern University visited the

Museum every day for specially designed tours. Nielsen's specific duty was to introduce the basic principles of the physical sciences to soldiers assigned to the Army Signal Corps Training School in Chicago. "We had a sense that this work was very important," said Lucy Nielsen Nedzel years later. "But it was also very difficult. The ideas were complicated, and it seemed like these groups were just racing through the Museum."

She prepared a number of short lectures. One of these, a favorite of Nielsen's, was on astronomy, crucial to the Signal Corps because of their work in navigation. "For this we didn't have a planetarium," she said. "I remember waving my arms around at the plaster ceilings." Another aspect of her rapid-fire physics course was electromagnetic radiation. Microwaves, on the short wave end of the electromagnetic spectrum, were responsible for radar, she explained. (This was to become one of the technologies that ultimately helped win the war.) To demonstrate invisible microwaves, Nielsen used a large glass prism filled with sulphur dioxide. It created a rainbow of colors, the approximate middle of the spectrum. She then asked the soldiers to imagine waves of radiation beyond the frequency of visible light. "I could only hope that they left understanding that light, radio waves, and radar were all parts of the same phenomenon. It was up to someone else to teach them what to do with it."

As thousands of trainees witnessed her demonstrations, Nielsen began to recognize just how much could be taught by the Museum of Science and Industry. It led to the topic of her doctoral research. With the support of the Museum and the full encouragement of her professors at the university, she decided to delve into the educational role of museums for a mass audience. She continued to read widely on museums and on known factors that separated people who enjoyed learning from those who normally did not. She assiduously recorded her observations as a demonstrator. Ultimately, she designed an entirely new portion of the Museum's physical science exhibit, the *Magnetism Room*, featuring diagrams, push buttons, live demonstrations and carefully worded labels. This was all described in her Ph.D. thesis, "The Motivation and Education of the General Public Through Museum Experiences."

While her research was in progress, Nielsen produced a number of shorter papers on modern museum techniques. One, "Action in Museum Education: Suggestions for Creating a Scientific Public," began by noting that too many people believed that museums were numbingly dull. Most institutions "conjure mental images of vast, musty halls, in which carefully arranged collections are arrayed endlessly on either side of dimly lit aisles." Too often it made teaching futile. "As long as educators and the public at large persist in regarding all museums in this light, those few museums who are trying to live down this tradition, and as Dana put it, devote themselves to service rather than acquisition and conservation, will find their seeds falling on stony ground."

Lohr found Lucy Nielsen's language highbrow. She believed he was more of a huckster than a scholar. But after a while they became unlikely allies.

Nielsen was convinced that a museum really could be a "school" in the ancient Greek sense of this word: "the utilization of leisure for study and meditation, as befits the citizens of a democracy," she wrote. Lohr was committed to an objective that turned out to be very similar—reaching a public whose attention span proved time and time again to be painfully short.

To apply her ideas at the Museum, Nielsen designed the *Magnetism Room* in a small stretch of corridor leading to the West Pavilion. The challenge, she knew, was formidable. "There appears to be an enduring dichotomy between people who are educationally motivated and those who are not," Nielsen wrote in her dissertation. Her objective was to overcome that dichotomy and teach average Museum visitors something of the importance of magnetism in their daily lives.

The exhibit consisted of six bays, each one tackling relatively simple scientific points in a logical sequence. One lesson was about magnetic poles, another on why magnets attract iron. Further on was a demonstration of what makes electric motors move. Several parts of the exhibit had buttons to push or rheostats to turn. Ultimately, Nielsen believed, someone willing to absorb information in all six bays could come away with the story of magnetism.

Most valuable in Nielsen's exhibit was something that could not be seen. It was her evaluation of it. In this period at the University of Chicago, scientific testing and evaluation were making considerable strides. This was a strong keynote of Hutchins' "core curriculum" theory, which was introduced shortly after he arrived in 1929. (The Great Books program was a related innovation.) Perhaps the second most important person at the university at this time was Dr. Ralph Tyler, a statistician hired to find out what students were learning and how long it took them to learn it. By the time Nielsen began her doctoral work, Tyler had become dean of the school of education and was clearly the inspiration behind her museum research.

Among her evaluation techniques, Nielsen used time-lapse photography to determine how long people remained in certain bays, and through additional testing she could determine the connection between the time spent there and the knowledge acquired. Among her many findings was that there was a ceiling to this relationship—after a certain point, increased time in an exhibit did not improve comprehension. Other findings related to the value of interactive devices—buttons to push and dials to turn. Those who used them really did come away with more.

Another point in Nielsen's analysis was subtle, but it proved to be one of her most important insights about museums. People who found the *Magnetism Room* by themselves were more successful in learning the subject than people who were asked to visit for the purpose of her survey. From this she deduced something basic about what makes people learn—that relaxed and unescorted visitors do best at opening their minds and letting information flow in. "We found out that a museum has to seek a balance between directing visitors to the lessons and letting them discover them on their own," said Nielsen. "We found out that museum work is an extremely delicate thing."

OTHERS ON LOHR'S STAFF were also paying attention to what made visitors respond. Arthur F. Pare, the Museum's chief demonstrator at that time, reported in a study that penetrating the visitor's mind was no easy matter. "Meeting the public requires more than simply a gracious manner and an engaging smile," Pare wrote. "It is a job that demands not a little courage of the beginner, a comparative amount of diplomacy and a superlative amount of patience."

In his observations, Pare found that the typical visitor group at the Museum was a family, and that different members of the average family came with different expectations. Boys were the most enthusiastic. They often led the family into the building and often ran ahead to the largest and most intriguing piece of machinery in sight. Girls were more reticent. "They do not become enthusiastic over specific exhibits, as do the boys," said Pare's study, which was made into a handbook for Museum demonstrators. Fathers frequently took pride in their knowledge of certain exhibits—farm equipment, for example, or machine tools. And mothers were typically torn between keeping up with their sons and staying within earshot of a demonstrator, assuming that this was the best way to comprehend the activity all around them. With all this going on, reaching the typical family was a challenge for any museum.

Some people, Pare found, were extremely eager to learn. "A family group from out of town perhaps enjoys these visits more than any other class. They listen attentively, are a receptive audience, and are quiet and reserved without the many inhibitions that might spoil their good time." Others were harder nuts to crack. "The other extreme in visitors is the local young man on a visit with his girl friend. He will not stop long in any one place, but tends to wander about, giving things but a superficial glance. If you want to be helpful, you find an approach almost impossible, because in most cases he has just finished explaining to the young lady his version of how a device operates and, of course, he prefers to retire in haste rather than risk the possibility of an explanation that might not coincide with his!"

What became obvious to Lohr and his staff was that not all visitors were equal, and that if anything could assure learning by the average visitor, it was a measure of advance preparation. That was one reason for the Museum's work to establish programs with the public schools in Chicago and in districts around the area. This program began with much promise, as the Chicago school superintendent, William H. Johnson, appointed a committee of administrators to coordinate activities between elementary classes and the Museum. School groups prepared for visits with lessons on aviation, navigation and even deep sea salvage. This often made all the difference. "The younger generation is quicker to get the main idea than are older folks," Pare discovered. "This, I think, is due largely to the fact that [most adults] cannot be properly amazed at anything."

So began a long-term love affair between the Museum and schoolchildren throughout the Chicago area. In 1942, when the Museum of Science and Industry reached its long-awaited one million mark in annual attendance, school groups contributed over 25,000 visitors that year. The attendance and the percentage of schoolchildren continued to increase almost every year for decades thereafter.

IN MANY WAYS, the first years of Major Lohr's tenure stabilized the Museum of Science and Industry. Financially the Museum was close to breaking even, due in part to a $120,000 museum tax, long discussed and finally levied by the park district shortly after Lohr arrived.

Yet the long-term prospects for an effective museum were still cloudy. In her dissertation, Lucy Nielsen worried that Lohr's planned reliance on corporate exhibitors was dangerous. She wrote "the majority of public relations offices responsible for such presentations are so deeply obsessed by the curse attached to the word 'education' in the public mind that they do not wish to consider sponsoring any presentation which is educational, regardless of how attractive it may be made to seem." She believed that corporations would have only one thing in mind: advertising.

It was up to Lohr to prove what continued to look like a dubious idea in his first several years at the Museum. It was the idea that mass education, which the Museum was beginning to master, was a good investment for private enterprise.

NINE

The Postwar Boom

The war effort made big corporate sponsorship impossible, but with victory in 1945, many American industries were poised for growth and eager to tell their stories. Lohr knew this. The Japanese had not been defeated long before he sent his right-hand man, Daniel MacMaster, along with smooth-talking salesman Paul Massmann, to Detroit to discuss the Museum of Science and Industry with General Motors Corporation.

Massmann was confident. He had worked with Lohr in 1933 to promote A Century of Progress and was seasoned at enticing corporate executives to sign up for exhibits. The younger MacMaster, however, was slightly nervous. He had a sheaf of tentative plans and renderings for a modest auto exhibit as imagined by in-house Museum designers. It was also MacMaster's job to explain that "advertising" was not permitted in Museum of Science and Industry exhibits. This meant that whatever need GM had to promote its products would have to be imbedded in something educational.

To MacMaster's relief, and as Massmann had expected, General Motors greeted them with open arms. The war had created a pent-up demand for autos. The manufacturer knew that the public would not need much coaxing to buy. Thus the men from the GM public relations department listened carefully as Massmann explained that tens of thousands of visitors flocked to the Museum every week. They nodded when MacMaster showed them the floor plan and drawings, which the GM men asked to keep.

MacMaster and Massmann were pleased and hoped that their meeting might come to something. Back in Chicago, Lohr was certain that it would. The Major, a marketing guru if there ever was one, understood that America's love affair with the automobile was only beginning, and that people would come to an exhibit that could unlock a few of its mysteries.

THERE WAS, IN FACT, no subject that Lohr regarded as quite so intriguing as the automobile. It represented the most powerful combination of technology and marketing the world had ever known—and thus a subject of supreme interest to the ultimate promoter of technology. Lohr was himself an antique car collector, with a garage full of early machines at his house in Evanston. And in 1945, when he was invited to speak in England before the learned engineers of the Newcomen Society, he naturally chose the automobile as his subject. No other invention in the history of man had evolved so swiftly. He marveled at how completely the industry was standardized, with internal combustion engines, sliding gear transmissions and water-cooled radiators.

How different it might have been! Witness, Lohr said in his speech, the very first automobile race in America, which, he was proud to say, had taken place in Chicago—the fabled *Times-Herald* Race of 1895. Finding entrants at that early date in automotive history had not been easy. The starting line saw six—four gasoline-powered machines and two electric. Several steam carriages and even some spring-powered ones that had also been promised to compete for the $5,000 purse did not show up. This was just as well, because the start was preceded by a fierce November snowstorm that was unkind to man, beast and certainly any primitive automobile. Confidence was in short supply that morning, but not just because of the weather. "In 1895," Lohr said, "nothing had been crystallized, the field was wide open to the imagination and inventive genius of all who would have a try."

The legacy of inventive genius, along with more than a modicum of Lohr's own showmanship, was behind his decision to restage the *Times-Herald* Race earlier in 1945. This was a 50th anniversary event with a gaggle of old and new cars on the same course—Hyde Park to Evanston and back. It was a noisy but picturesque spectacle. One of Lohr's goals in the race (more a parade than a race, he said) and the point of his Newcomen talk was to show that there were many types of automobiles on the road before the industry came to its standard design. "Is the car of today the best that could have evolved from the multitude of ideas and inventions that were tried?" Lohr wondered. Other approaches had been feasible a half century before and probably still were. Electric batteries were now longer-lasting; steam was powerful but probably required more "constant attention and skillful handling" than most drivers were willing to give.

Most of all, of course, Lohr's 50th anniversary race was a crowd pleaser. Spectators saw not only the old machines but later models as well. There was a 1909 Sears, Roebuck mail-order model (Lohr's own), an amphibious Marine

America's first automobile race took place in Chicago in 1895 when the *Times-Herald* Race started and ended at the building that would become the Museum of Science and Industry. The original race was won by J. Frank Duryea (above wearing bowler) in a gas-powered car that was regarded as the country's first production automobile. Duryea returned to Chicago in 1945 (below at right with early Chicago automobilist Ruben DeLaunty) for a 50th anniversary of the original race organized by Museum president Lenox Lohr.

Corps Weasel from World War II, and nearly 30 others in between. All this was designed to bring the curious (and news photographers) to the Museum of Science and Industry for the start and finish. The event featured an automobile celebrity, J. Frank Duryea, then 76 years old, who 50 years before had won the Chicago race in his own 1895-model Duryea. And there was even a tinge of controversy. This involved Duryea's nephew, M. J. Duryea, who drove another car in the event and complained to anyone who would listen that he was tired of Uncle Frank taking credit for the success of the early Duryea auto manufacturing business, recognized as America's first. M. J. claimed that his father, Charles, who had died in 1930, was the real brains behind the country's earliest commercial car. The controversy has been since resolved in Frank's favor, but it was an interesting sidelight in a prominent story in the next day's *Chicago Tribune*.

HISTORY, OF COURSE, belongs to those who survive and flourish. Accordingly, when the Museum convinced General Motors to put in a major installation, it invited the company to design and furnish its own exhibit and tell the story of the automobile from its own point of view. While Museum ground rules discouraged self-promotion, *Motorama*, as the exhibit was called, chronicled the role of the automobile in the progress of American life.

Automobile technology was not always simple, but the company's message of progress was loud and clear. In one streamlined exhibit case, *Motorama* displayed Johannsen Blocks, the primitive but absolutely essential measuring instruments that had made interchangeable parts and the mass production of automobiles possible. Other snippets of auto history included the story of the ignition system. Visitors could test a starter crank like the one used in a 1912 Buick, which was hard work and at one time liable to kick back. The "self-starter," it was explained, was introduced in 1914, and *Motorama* included the very first car off the assembly line with such a device. It was a Cadillac V-8 that had been traced back to Sault Sainte Marie, Ontario, where it was originally delivered to carry the Prince of Wales in a ceremony to open a new section of locks at the Sault.

Whereas the Museum of Science and Industry remained focused on the future, there was something about automotive history that was beginning to tug at American nostalgia at this time. Next to *Motorama*, therefore, GM added *Yesterday's Main Street*, a dramatically lit corner of old Chicago with cobblestones, an old tin lizzie (visitor portraits were posed behind the wheel), full-size storefronts and even a nickelodeon. The message beneath the surface of this exhibit was that autos and American cities had grown up together and were designed for each other.

GM naturally exhibited their newest and latest models as well, but the real drawing card of the auto exhibit was not *Motorama* at all but the antique

Beginning in 1941, the Museum conducted Christmastime ceremonies honoring the American military and its allies during World War II. Pictured here is an observance commemorating United States Day, 1944. The custom continued after the war and soon became *Christmas Around the World*, an annual festival and the Museum's most popular event.

and vintage cars. Because of the Major's own interest, the Museum assembled quite a collection around this time, getting involved before prices got out of hand. A friend of Lohr's, wealthy dairy owner and auto collector Cameron Peck, became the unpaid curator of transportation at the Museum.

Local auto enthusiasts recall that many of Peck's and Lohr's own antiques went into the Museum collection in the early 1940s to protect them from mandatory scrap-metal laws during World War II, when there was little appreciation for old cars outside of a small group of collectors. The Museum became a perfect place to do what would not be tolerated today—run an active business for cars and parts among members of the local chapter of the Antique Automobile Club.

Eventually, many of Lohr's and Peck's cars, and a few from their friends, were passed permanently to the Museum. To their credit, the permanent collection left behind chronicled several important turns in automobile history. Its curved-dash Olds, 1904, was built with a hint of early styling and resemblance to a fashionable but conventional horse-drawn carriage. A pair of Model Ts, on the other hand, came a bit later but were as basic and mass-producible as Henry Ford could make them.

In time, the Museum's car collection would also include automotive symbols of excess wealth. A 1929 Dussenberg represented America's most luxurious, not to say advanced, piece of engineering at the time. A 1929 Rolls Royce that came to the collection had a near-royal pedigree. Belonging to the family of Chicagoan William McCormick Blair, it logged miles in every one of the nation's 48 states before its retirement.

BEFORE THEY SPENT hundreds of thousands of dollars on an exhibit at the Museum of Science and Industry, corporations needed assurance of high visitorship. For this reason, attendance was constantly on the mind of the Lenox Lohr regime, and his staff studied the figures constantly. The raw numbers were impressive—1,666,454 were recorded in 1949. Other visitor data were generated to make the Museum ever more attractive to corporate dollars, and when survey results could be digested in a single gulp, they were always given to the newspapers. A 1950 report, for example, showed that the average visit to the Museum had increased in length phenomenally—from 30 minutes in 1940 to 3 1/2 hours ten years later. The Museum of Science and Industry was indisputably the city's most popular cultural attraction. Potential exhibitors could calculate for themselves that the money they put into it was well spent.

Knowing that attendance figures were the Museum's lifeblood, Lohr was constantly encouraging new populations of Chicagoans to visit the Museum. One such group was schoolchildren. They were a natural constituency but always required special attention and coaxing. So Lohr sent Dan MacMaster out to the schools to give talks before children of all ages. MacMaster talked

At *Christmas Around the World,* many of Chicago's ethnic communities come to the Museum to celebrate the holidays in their own traditional ways. Here, a group of Chinese Americans perform Christmas carols at the festival in 1946.

about the *Coal Mine*, naturally, and other exhibits that explained the business of everyday life, such as International Harvester's farm exhibit and Illinois Bell's telephones in a hall next to the *Whispering Gallery*. He also buttonholed their teachers, insisting that the Museum specialized in making the lessons of technology interesting for everyone. "If the student hasn't learned, the teacher hasn't taught," he kept saying.

Success in the schools was matched by steady growth in attendance among other groups who were otherwise unaccustomed to large cultural institutions. "Many ethnic groups in Chicago felt that they weren't welcomed in the big museums on the lakefront," MacMaster said years later. "We wanted to change that." One of the first efforts to reach out to ethnic Chicago actually came during World War II, when the Museum agreed to help restore and exhibit an old Polish sloop called the *Dal*. Polish sailors had sailed this boat to Chicago in 1933 from Gdynia, Poland for A Century of Progress. The vessel had been moored on the lakefront since then and was in bad condition. With Lohr's prompting, the Polish Roman Catholic Union organized a troop of Sea Scouts to do the restoration work. When the sloop was presented to the Museum, it stood as a symbol of Polish resistance to the Nazi occupation. It started a continuous flow of Chicago Poles to the Museum of Science and Industry.

Another effort to bring Chicago's many ethnic groups into the Museum at that time quickly became Lohr's most successful yearly event ever—*Christmas Around the World*. Starting in 1941 as United Nations Day, a salute to America's allies during the war, it grew into a unique and nationally famous festival. Whereas most museums tended to be relatively empty during the holidays, *Christmas Around the World* made December the Museum's most popular month.

Christmas trees were the natural centerpiece of this event. In the first year, there were a dozen such trees decorated in various national styles. A few years later more than 40 conifers filled the exhibit hall. Initially the Museum attempted to blend a technological message with holiday cheer. An exhibit called "Science Behind Santa" used inflatable balls to illustrate elasticity and used sleds to provide lessons in friction. Very quickly, however, Museum officials realized that dance and music performances by local ethnic groups were the event's biggest draw. On one occasion a skit by a troupe of local Dutch Americans brought Saint Nicholas on stage atop a fine white steed that was coaxed into the theater down ramps and up an elevator.

Diplomatic as always, the Museum was careful to separate potentially hostile ethnic groups. The trees of Serbs and Croats, for instance, were placed at reasonable distance from one another. Other international situations were duly noted and avoided. (The Germans were invited only after the end of World War II.) Serious trouble never materialized, but the proceedings were monitored. At one celebration in the '50s, a group from a central European country performed colorful dances and wonderful songs, after which a man rose to speak on the religious significance of the holiday. Unfortunately, his remarks were distinctly anti-Semitic. Martha McGrew, Lohr's faithful director of operations, quickly caught wind of the incident and made certain that nothing like it was repeated. Her iron hand prevailed, and the result was an annual extravaganza that was rarely anything but joyous.

THE MUSEUM OF SCIENCE AND INDUSTRY became a showcase for ethnic celebrations as well as for technological genius. This might have seemed like an unlikely mix for a museum, but it had a certain logic. The Museum's central theme, after all, was the American dream, and as the message dawned on corporations throughout the country, they were eager to be a part of it.

Another early exhibitor in the postwar years, Commonwealth Edison, created a major exhibit in 1951 entitled *Electric Theater*. It was dedicated to the proposition that electricity was one of the most remarkable inventions that ever

When Soviet Foreign Minister Vyacheslav M. Molotov (center) visited
Chicago in 1955, he came to the Museum of Science and Industry to
witness the real battlefield of the Cold War—technological progress. Here,
Museum president Lenox Lohr explains a point, with future Soviet leader
Leonid Brezhnev to the right of Molotov.

graced the American landscape. Not only was electric power responsible for
nearly every modern convenience of importance, its price was actually going
down. This was the story that executives at Commonwealth Edison and its sister utility, Public Service of Northern Illinois, wanted to tell. Museum rules
against advertising didn't dampen their enthusiasm. In *Electric Theater*, any
description of the wonders of modern American life could and did revolve
around electricity.

    "The whole idea was to make people feel good about electricity," said Her-
man Sereika, one of several Commonwealth Edison employees serving as mas-

ter of ceremonies when *Electric Theater* first opened. Sereika was a Commonwealth Edison lighting designer whose regular job it was to work with large electric customers. He was a specialist in lighting technology who helped businesses upgrade their lighting systems and ultimately sold them the use of more electric power. Sereika was a talented salesman. He often took his best prospects to Neela Park, the General Electric lighting laboratory in Ohio, to explain how illumination of the highest quality could be achieved.

Sereika was therefore a logical choice when the company needed amateur actors for *Electric Theater*. He was tall, handsome and bow-tied. He understood the technology and believed in the industry completely. The script that he and others developed for the Museum was always entertaining. "Scientists have discovered the secret of the firefly," he began his performance. "We now know that the firefly has special glands for secreting special chemicals." Whereupon he poured several compounds together into a vial and produced a faint glow. "There we have it! Chemical or firefly light—thousands of times as bright as the light of a single firefly. Yet you can't read a newspaper by it. And how expensive is it?" Sereika always smiled at this point. "Chemical light produced in this manner costs about 25 million times as much as light produced with electricity."

Sereika went on to describe in detail the wonders of electric lighting. He first demonstrated a replica of an Edison lamp, then a stroboscope that helped engineers develop fast-moving equipment such as turbines, and then even photoelectric cells that were better known as electric eyes. *Electric Theater* was not a simple performance. It covered some concepts that were very complex for the average museum visitor. Yet Sereika got through the fundamentals, such as the electromagnetic spectrum—which included electric waves and X-rays—and pointed out that it also included radio waves. Radio waves were used in one of the more curious features in his presentation. It was an oven that could cook a turkey in a few minutes, not hours. It was a big, clunky thing and required 750 volts. But it worked. It was an early microwave oven.

CONSUMERISM WAS NOW THE KEYNOTE of American life. It was also prominent in most major exhibits in the Museum of Science and Industry during this period. Its presentation was accompanied by a large measure of patriotism just underneath the surface. "In these days of world change," Lohr once said, "it becomes increasingly important that the fundamentals of American democracy be portrayed. The Museum has but one thing to sell—the truth, and the eternal verities."

The Museum was on course. Evidence for this was the attention sometimes generated when Communist visitors passed through the city and could not resist a look at the Museum of Science and Industry. One of the most important such visitors came in 1955—Soviet Foreign Minister Vyacheslav M. Molo-

In the postwar economic boom years, many large American industries
were eager to participate in programs at the Museum. Here, a demonstrator in an exhibit sponsored by B. F. Goodrich shows how hard rubber
is fashioned from latex and an acid solution.

tov, whose motorcade endured a series of demonstrations en route to the
Museum. Molotov was followed by newsmen during his tour as he viewed
exhibits about technological progress, which the Russians and Americans both
acknowledged was the Cold War's real battlefield. In silence he made mental
notes, comparing American progress with that of his own country. There was little for him to say as he saw lavish, sparkling exhibits that obviously outdid anything that was on public display in the Soviet Union. Molotov brightened only
when a cooperative reporter called out and asked him if he had seen Chicago's
slums. Yes, he replied through his interpreter, these were the true "historic land-
marks" of America.

EVERY TIME A NEW EXHIBIT was introduced, corporate heads flocked to the presentation ceremony which Lohr aptly made into a grand production. Such events were always a pleasant experience for executives, because the Museum of Science and Industry had become an unabashed shrine of American capitalism. One of the more poignant exhibit openings of this period took place in 1950, when the People's Gas Company christened the *Story of Flame Gas*. This exhibit featured intricate models and detailed descriptions of the vast pipeline system from the gas fields of Texas to the compressor stations in Chicago.

Among the speakers on this occasion was a man unconnected to the gas industry, but a pillar of the local business community, Chicago railroad executive Ralph Budd. Budd noted in his speech that the gas exhibit was an excellent representation of the strength and reach of American enterprise. Indeed, the Museum should continue to have exhibits like it, and the message on behalf of such sponsors should, if anything, be stronger.

"Free enterprise is an economic commodity that must be sold in the competitive marketplace," Budd said. "Let's face the fact that we have not advertised it as such for a long, long time. . . .The American way of life is products, commodities—more things for more people at less cost . . . and above all, more freedom to live with our individual consciences."

There was applause. For his part, Lohr showed little emotion when Ralph Budd sat down. What might have sounded like a challenge to the Museum was not at all far from the Lohrian view of the world. The truth was that if they could put Budd's speech to music, it would have been the anthem of the Museum of Science and Industry, which was determined to become the true "historic landmark" of the economic expansion that was only just beginning.

TEN

Chicago's Greatest Showman

Chicago was always an excitable city. In Lenox Lohr, it had a great ringmaster.

Lohr's skill as a showman came through again when he was recruited to take time from his Museum duties to organize the Chicago Railroad Fair. It was 1948, and Chicago was determined to celebrate its centenary of railroading, harking back to 1848, when the tiny locomotive called the Pioneer puffed five miles out from the city and back. Despite the importance of this milestone, Mayor Martin Kennelly knew that getting cooperation for the event would be no easy matter. Chicago railroads had a history of ruthless competition. Even in recent years, many had resisted all efforts to consolidate in a new station that would untangle streets in the south Loop.

For this reason, Kennelly asked Lohr to direct the fair, to which the Major agreed, but only under strict conditions. One was that he would have full control; there would be no meddling by the executives or by politicians. Another was that staff members from the Museum would be hired for daily management of the event—principally Dan MacMaster, who was made executive officer. This was agreed, and Lohr and company immediately had a chance to prove their organizational mettle. They overcame what was admittedly a late start in construction by jumping into action and building a rail spur across Lake Shore Drive to the fair site at 23rd Street in a single night.

Lohr went on to explain to the railroad executives that if the fair were lavish, exotic and colorful, Chicagoans would come. His idea was to salute the entire history of American railroads with an emphasis on the important destinations of the past. Within a few months, Illinois Central replicated a section of the French Quarter of New Orleans, with grilled balconies, hidden courtyards and shady cafes. Santa Fe spent hundreds of thousands of dollars on a Southwestern Indian Village where Native Americans performed dances and worked on traditional crafts.

Very much in the Lohr style, the Railroad Fair had a big opening celebration with a parade in the Loop and a grand marshal that everyone wanted to see. She was Janie B. Jones, Mrs. Casey Jones, 80 years old and a pint-sized packet of energy who smoked innumerable cigarettes and preferred Scotch whiskey straight up. She retold the story of her late husband's death in a legendary crash on April 30, 1900. When she saw the fair exhibits she said, "Only wish Casey could be here. But I don't know what he'd think of these new diesels with their astrodomes and stuff."

The Railroad Fair ran for two summers, and both years its biggest attraction by far was the pageant production entitled *Wheels a-Rolling*. This was an hour-long performance with singing, dancing and full-size trains rolling in on tracks to tell the story of transportation and our nation. Written by the "dean of American railroad writers," Edward Hungerford, who had penned a similar show for the New York World's Fair in 1939, it was a hit. Some out-of-town critics were fussy, of course. Lucius Beebe of the *New York Herald-Tribune* complained that the driving of the Golden Spike—when East was finally connected to West by continuous rail—was staged with music so solemn that it seemed religious "instead of being depicted as it was in fact, one of the booziest and most hilarious events remembered by the old West." Historically correct or not, *Wheels a-Rolling* was performed four times every day, and the lakefront grandstand was filled to bursting much of the time.

The show's most remarkable notice came from the *Chicago Tribune*'s Claudia Cassidy, the most acerbic and feared critic ever in Chicago. In Cassidy's career, she single-handedly chased at least one conductor of the Chicago Symphony Orchestra out of town and had dozens of other notches on her blunderbuss. But of *Wheels a-Rolling* she was a true and unexpected booster. "This is really quite a show," she wrote. "You can gaze with admiration at the fabulous 'Train of Tomorrow' or lose your heart to the lively and somehow flirtatious little engine known as Chief Crazy Horse. . . . Actually pageant seems a static word for so mobile a production. Time flies on wheels from oxcarts to sleek diesel. . . . It is a wonderful display of authentic conveyances past and present, and it manages to be amusing, touching, and exciting."

LOHR WAS A MILITARY ENGINEER, outwardly taciturn and serious. But he understood and loved entertainment. Guests to his large house in Evanston, for example, were always invited to the small theater in his basement after dinner. Old movies, it turned out, were his hobby, and the silent ones were his favorites. So it was as a genuine fan that Lohr greeted a succession of movie and stage stars to the Railroad Fair and made a particular point of meeting

Colleen Moore, the great screen star of the silent era, had been adding to her famous *Fairy Castle* for decades when President Lenox Lohr convinced her to place it permanently in the Museum of Science and Industry. Moore's elaborate fantasy house included the slippers of Cinderella, paintings of Mickey and Minnie Mouse and even books by authors such as F. Scott Fitzgerald and Sir Arthur Conan Doyle.

Colleen Moore, the great film star of the era before the talkies. Lohr invited her to lunch in the director's private dining car.

Lohr and Moore had plenty to talk about. They chatted about her films, such as *Flaming Youth* and *Lilac Time*. Typically, Lohr quickly moved the conversation to a subject that might benefit his Museum. What he had on his mind specifically was Moore's Fairy Castle. This dollhouse represented the longtime and famous hobby of the actress and also a staggering bit of craftsmanship. Its Great Central Hall, for example, was constructed with extravagant gothic vaults. A perfect replica of Bernini's *Pluto and Persephone* stood before a wall of intricately etched glass. Nearby were hung thumbnail-sized paintings of greats from Moore's own imagination, such as Mickey and Minnie Mouse in the garb of the King and Queen of Hearts.

It took years for set designers, miniaturists and others to design and build the castle for Miss Moore, whose stories about her hobby were often as wonderful as the objects themselves. For a pair of Cinderella's glass slippers, for example, she traveled all over the world in search of a glassblower to undertake the task. She went to Venice but found no one who could promise the intricate detail she demanded. Her quest finally ended in Jackson, Michigan, where a skilled German artisan reduced the magical slippers to a size one-quarter-inch long.

What was hidden in the *Fairy Castle* was just as important to Colleen Moore as what was visible. In the castle's drawing room, for example, the music on the piano was handwritten, it was said, by the composers themselves. Rachmaninoff made a version of "Prelude" as a special favor to the actress. Gershwin gave her the tiniest copy of "Rhapsody in Blue" ever, and to fill her library she obtained dozens of tiny tomes with leather bindings and blank pages. Moore had friends who were also authors write in a few lines by hand. Edgar Rice Burroughs wrote a complete *Tarzan* story. Daphne Du Maurier penned the famous first sentence of *Rebecca*. Sir Arthur Conan Doyle, Sinclair Lewis, F. Scott Fitzgerald and other popular writers are also represented.

Other whimsical stories revolved around the castle's "regal chambers," a bedroom with a floor of mother-of-pearl and a bed shaped like a gilded skiff. Several pieces for this room came into being after Moore visited a jeweler of her acquaintance. "Those dress clips you're wearing would make beautiful chairs for a princess," the jeweler told her. So they did. The chambers also had a miniature "polar bear rug" made from a tiny piece of ermine. Moore asked if the rug could be made with the mouth wide open like a bear's. The maker hesitated but finally finished it with wicked white teeth. "I caught a little mouse," he said, "took out his teeth and put them in your polar bear."

Since Colleen Moore's Fairy Castle had long traveled around the country to benefit children's charities, Lohr quickly fixed on an idea he hoped would be appealing. Her castle, he acknowledged, was an effective fund-raiser, but the Museum of Science and Industry could give all children a chance to see the amazing house for free. The actress could only agree. She later described her dining-car negotiations with the Major as something between swift and instantaneous. The subject of her castle came up as they were served the soup course, she said. "By the time dessert was served, he had the dollhouse!"

THE WORD "BLOCKBUSTER" had not yet been applied to museums, but Lohr kept producing them. Another such triumph grew from his idea to have the American Society of Engineers convene at the Museum of Science and Industry for its centennial-year meeting in 1952. This was a big group—30,000 engineers, most of whom were from out of town—and Lohr took the notion a step further. He became producer of a musical comedy designed primarily for the engineers, but which eventually brought in some 60,000 people and ran for two months. It got the Museum the kind of publicity that normally went to Loop theaters and North Side nightclubs. It even rated a color spread in *Life* magazine.

The play was *From Adam to Atom*, a humorous and colorful story of human ingenuity from the dawn of mankind. It was a huge production, with 70 performers playing the roles of 400 characters. The play began with a bit about the day that ape-men discovered fire; the discovery occurred when a bolt of lightning stuck a tree outside their drafty cave. The resulting fire looked like just another natural disaster until one of the residents had the genius to bring a small flame inside. Other scenes ran quickly through the centuries, with a revolving stage that moved briskly from the pyramid builders to Eli Whitney to the automobile. In staging the building of the Panama Canal, the burdens of the world's largest earthmoving operation were lightened somewhat by the appearance of lovely flamenco dancers.

Lest *From Adam to Atom* be taken as just another headline for hoofers, the ever-serious Major called journalists in to explain to them why the Museum was getting into this kind of entertainment. It was to promote engineering, a much neglected profession at the time. "We must succeed in reaching the youngsters by showing them the glamour and necessity of this profession," he said without cracking a smile. For whatever reason, the people came. The show's success, it might be assumed, was due in part to the modern air-conditioning in the West Pavilion theater. But mostly, big ticket sales—the tickets cost $1.25 for adults and 60 cents for children—corresponded with rave reviews that equaled those of the other hit show in Chicago that year, *Stalag 17*.

LOHR'S GREATEST SPECTACLE was yet to come. It combined his background as a military man, his knack for technical problems and his utter audacity in staging events that should have seemed impossible. It was the arrival of the U-505, an 840-ton German submarine that was lifted across Lake Shore Drive on the night of September 3, 1954.

An amazing sequence of events led to that climactic event. They began, one could say, in August 1941, when the German *Unterseeboot*, U-505, was commissioned with much fanfare in Hamburg. This was a moment when prospects for a Nazi victory seemed very high indeed, largely because of the ability of U-boats to disrupt English supply lines. The fleet had grown to approximately 1,000 submarines, and their plan to demoralize the allies appeared to be working.

The U-505 itself got off to a lucky start. In early 1942, after training in the Baltic Seas, it sailed for patrols near the French West African coast and quickly sank four English freighters. It then crossed to the Caribbean, where it sank three more ships, two of them American. But then its good fortune seemed to run out. In November 1942, the U-505 was hit by an American bomb in an air attack that damaged the sub sufficiently to send it to Lorient, France, for repairs.

From then on, life for the U-boat's crew was an ordeal. Allied ships were faster now. American aircraft were better at stalking, and as often as not, the U-505 was the attacked and not the attacker. Then on June 4, 1944, again off French West Africa, its fateful battle began. The USS *Chatelain*, part of an American submarine-hunting task force, made initial sonar contact with the U-505, at which point Captain Daniel V. Gallery, commanding the flagship USS *Guadalcanal*, sent Wildcat fighters overhead to follow the submarine and mark its position. A barrage of depth charges followed, until one of the planes radioed back: "You struck oil! Sub is surfacing."

Actually, the U-505 was lucky to surface. One charge made a direct hit. The sub's lights went out, according to a German crew member, and it began to drop like a rock. Fortunately, its air pipes were still in order, and the submarine surfaced and disgorged its crew. They were met by a torrent of machine gun fire, killing one German officer, until the crew fully surrendered.

This completed only part of Gallery's work. Before going out on his "hunter-killer" mission, he told superiors that he was determined to capture a German submarine. It would be a first, since U-boats on the losing end of battles were either sunk by depth charges or intentionally scuttled by their crew. Seizing a German submarine intact, said Gallery, might yield great amounts of military intelligence. So when the Germans came topside, the Americans were ready. Several of Gallery's sailors jumped aboard the sub. Some of them quickly collected the ship's records. Others searched for booby traps, and then closed the single sea valve that the German crew had had time to open. The Americans were successful, and this became the Navy's first high-seas capture of an enemy vessel since the War of 1812.

Gallery hooked the submarine to a towline and started for Dakar on the African Coast, the closest friendly port. He was quickly diverted, however, because Dakar was riddled with spies who could report back to Berlin on the capture, and the intelligence from the sub would be valuable only if the German command believed the U-505 was safely at the bottom of the sea. Gallery turned around and went to Bermuda instead, where the ship could be studied in absolute secrecy.

The story of the dramatic capture of the U-505 was made public only after the war in Europe was over. It was then that Lohr also learned that the hero of the operation, Daniel Gallery, was a Chicagoan. Immediately, the Major set the wheels in motion to bring the U-505 to the Museum, and in 1948 he prevailed upon a U.S. senator to introduce an act of Congress to permit it. This was done, and all that was left at that point was to raise the money to get it to Chicago and restore it.

For the next few years, the U-505 was a cause célèbre among civic leaders in Chicago. Fund-raising events were held. The film *Away Boarders*, shot by Navy filmmakers during the actual battle, was frequently shown. Gallery

The final voyage of the U-505 in 1954 was completed when the submarine was put on rollers and rails and pulled across Lake Shore Drive en route to its perch outside the Museum's East Pavilion.

himself, then an admiral at Glenview Naval Air Station, appeared in the film and explained in technical detail the capture and analysis of German decoding equipment and the acoustic torpedoes, technologies that had confounded allied shipping earlier in the war. Neutralizing these was critical, he said, in overcoming the U-boat threat and eventually beating the Germans.

Ultimately, more than $200,000 was donated, and the U-505 began its trip from Portsmouth, New Hampshire, where it had been mothballed, through the Saint Lawrence Seaway to Lake Michigan. The voyage was made in the spring of 1954 by towboat, and most of the journey was uneventful. It was the last 800 feet, from the 57th Street beach to the U-505's eventual perch beside the Museum's east wall, that was trickiest.

The problem was solved by raising the sub—all 840 tons of it—on a floating dry dock and moving it on rollers and iron rails across the sand and Lake Shore Drive. It was done overnight to minimize traffic tie-ups on the Drive, then Chicago's busiest highway. Despite the hour, the U-505 drew a throng of spectators that night, and continued to draw them for years thereafter as one of the Museum of Science and Industry's most important icons.

Miracles of Communications

No other technology revealed the soul of the 20th century quite like the machines invented for communications. From the time the Museum of Science and Industry opened, curators sought ways to demonstrate the fundamentals of the field and later kept up to date with exhibits on telephones, radios and broadcasting.

The Museum's fascination with modern communications went further. As the Museum explained its wonders to visitors, it also employed these technologies for its own public relations needs. The enthusiasm of Lohr and his staff about using modern communications as well as teaching the subject ultimately proved that philosopher and media expert Marshall McLuhan was right. The medium and the message had merged.

The Museum's earliest curators knew very well what was on the horizon. Some of the most important lessons of the Museum's first exhibits concerned the laws of electromagnetism and electronic communications. In the '30s, highlights in the Physics Hall included a stroboscope, oscilloscopes and vacuum tubes. Of course, translating principles into language understandable by the public was a knotty problem, and this proved to be a continuing challenge. The consensus, even inside the Museum, was that they often failed at showing why Hertzian waves created radio frequencies or how triode tubes led to radio and television reception. Even the *Whispering Gallery*, popular since it opened in 1938, often hit a brick wall when it came to complex lessons, even if people were fascinated by the way the faintest sound could be carried across a 30-ft. room.

It was maddening. Well into the '40s, the Museum's head curator, Dr. Harvey Lemon, whom Lohr brought from the physics department of the University of Chicago, reported that many scientific exhibits in the Museum simply did not teach what they set out to teach. "It appears that the present lack at the Museum of a complete sequential presentation of the fundamental principles, facts, and methods of study in both the physical and biological sciences is regarded as the major obstacle to profitable use of the Museum by serious minded and studiously inclined people," he wrote in a report. What he and others could not find at first was a bridge between difficult concepts and the people who seemed intent on breezing through the Museum.

Ultimately, the answer lay in Lohr's resolve to get industrial corporations actively involved. Business, certainly more than scholars, was adept at capturing public interest, and by the time World War II was over, it was evident that communications technology was one story that could best be told by people who had the job of actually selling it. This was first suggested in 1938, before Lohr's arrival, when Illinois Bell installed *Oscar the Dummy*, a demonstration that the phone company introduced in 1933 at A Century of Progress. Oscar sat in a glass-enclosed office with the audience sitting outside wearing headsets. As sounds were emitted inside—a pencil dropping or a voice whispering—visitors heard them via highly sensitive microphones in Oscar's two ears. The sensation was distinctly like being in the office and in Oscar's very location. The lesson—beyond demonstrating Bell's remarkable reproduction of sound—concerned binaural hearing and its importance in the human sense of place and distance.

With Oscar's success, the telephone exhibit was expanded. And as new Bell technologies were put on display, curators discerned that the people really were learning, sometimes despite their short attention spans. Moreover, Museum staff witnessed how the Museum and private industry could help one another. "Great care should be taken," longtime curator James Van Pelt wrote in a memo to Lemon, "to avoid any implication that standard telephones aren't as good as they could be." Most important was that the Museum had a demonstration of sound traveling across wires, while Bell Telephone enjoyed a public relations triumph.

The Museum's first serious foray into radio technology came just before the war ended, when companies were still prohibited by law from major promotional efforts. At this time, the Chicago company that made Motorola radio equipment was already talking to the Museum about coming in as soon as possible. The Galvin Manufacturing Company, later called Motorola, had been "working on various electronic devices for the government," Van Pelt wrote to Lemon. "They are making a lot of money and want to do something to keep the public from forgetting the name and their position in the radio industry. It looks as if they will be willing to spend $20,000 on architecture alone, and perhaps more than that on exhibits."

Oscar the Dummy (center) was brought to the Museum by Bell Telephone
in 1938. The *Oscar* exhibit used highly sensitive equipment to demonstrate
the surprising ways in which sound and hearing affect our lives.

Demonstrating how radios worked would be a challenge. Motorola's *Story of Radio*, which opened in 1946, was intended to explain how condensers stored up quantities of electronic charge and then released them to emit carrier waves. These charges, controlled by inductors and further altered by triode oscillators, traveled through space and then could be interpreted by a distant receiver. At this time, radio technology was already basic to people's lives, but once again, understanding it simply fell outside the realm of normal experience. The curators knew this and helped Galvin designers devise visitor-friendly push buttons and dials. With flickering lights, the exhibit illustrated the triode's role in voltage and sound amplification. Still, the lessons were hard. There were places in the exhibit where explanatory labels simply stated: "If you have difficulty understanding this, restudy the preceding exhibits," including those on magnetism and sound.

This frustrated serious scientists and teachers of science, who wanted above all to teach their courses in a cogent way. Yet Motorola drew visitors. This was because there were microphones to talk into and oscilloscopes to depict the transmitted voice. The meaning of such things may have remained fuzzy to most people. But real lessons were seeping through. Thoughtful visitors might discern, for example, the difference between "amplitude modulation" (AM) and "frequency modulation" (FM) radio. The explanation was that one band varied the power, or amplitude, of the wave on a constant frequency; the other varied or "modulated" the frequency of the signal to transmit sound across air.

The real attractions of the Motorola exhibit, of course, were the products themselves, and curators could only hope that displays of walkie-talkies and police-band radios would intrigue visitors enough to help them learn the scientific principles at stake. It continued to be a tough assignment. In December 1946, for example, Dr. Lemon was invited to discuss *The Story of Radio* on a 15-minute talk show. WGNB, a station with a cultural bent, was then one of the few FM outlets in the city and had a vested interest in educating the public about the improved clarity of FM. As always, it was hard to do more than scratch the surface. Lemon began by describing electromagnetism, which included radio waves and, at the far end of the spectrum, cosmic rays.

"Cosmic rays have something to do with atomic energy, haven't they?" asked the hostess of the show.

"Yes, it is the stray neutrons produced by cosmic rays that set off the fission of uranium in the atomic bomb," Lemon replied.

"It's hard for the layman to understand that radio and the atomic bomb have anything in common," the interviewer said. She then asked if Santa Claus might arrive electronically at some point in the future.

Lemon went along and joked that they might wrap Father Christmas in a carrier wave that would enable him to come in the house by way of the antenna on the roof, and not the chimney. It was pleasant repartee. It might have advanced the knowledge of radio a few small steps.

WHEN LENOX LOHR left the National Broadcasting Company for the Museum of Science and Industry, he was not giving up broadcasting as much as he was leaving David Sarnoff, the engineer-turned-businessman who had built the NBC empire. Sarnoff, later called the "General," was no bargain to work for. "I don't want anyone around as smart as I am," he once said.

Nevertheless, Lohr and Sarnoff were reunited (albeit loosely) in 1950, when NBC's parent company opened the RCA Victor Television Exhibit. This was an excellent match—the premier technician of radio and television with the master showman of modern technology. The RCA exhibit quickly became a must-see for the vast majority of the 70,000 people who visited the Museum each month. (Lohr's surveys indicated that 80 percent of his visitors saw the RCA exhibit, a statistic that was faithfully reported to the company.)

Despite the dazzle that RCA could provide, the serious lessons were still hard to teach. The exhibit began by explaining that the earliest television in the 1920s used spinning perforated disks in both the camera and the receiver. As blinking light from the object activated phototubes in the camera, frequency-modulated radio waves activated corresponding lamps in the picture tube. This spinning-disk system, of course, was cumbersome and of low quality. The exhibit went on to explain that RCA's great advance in television was the development of an electronic system. Instead of mechanically scanning the optical image, RCA scientist Dr. Vladimir Zworykin invented the technique of magnetic deflection, a way of bending an electron beam to traverse a 525-line screen 30 times per second. Instead of a spinning disk, this invention used a screen of sensors, a "raster," inside the camera. The raster transmitted the image to another screen inside the picture tube, coated with phosphors that would glow according to the impact of a corresponding beam of electrons.

Although the Museum was frequently confounded by difficulties in teaching television technology, there was cause for encouragement. Adults were sometimes confused by the exhibit's high level of technology, but it was often children who could reduce the exhibit to the essentials. "It's not that hard to understand, Dad," demonstrators often heard in the RCA gallery. Children would run over to a model that illustrated how baseball games were broadcast by an array of strategically positioned cameras. This would remind the adults of political conventions, first broadcast in 1948 with radio pioneer Edward R. Murrow doing the commentary. The large potential of television, if not the minutiae of its technology, became clear. Visitors young and old stopped at the small stage called "See Yourself by Television." They stood on the platform, swung their arms in front of the camera, and viewed their own live image on an actual television screen.

The real story of television lay in its ability to captivate the public. The General understood this. In the medium's early days, Sarnoff frequently said that resistance was inevitable (old-time telegraphers, after all, were convinced that Marconi's wireless radio would pass) but television would soon prevail. His remarks at the opening of the RCA exhibit were prophetic. "Television may determine the next President of the United States," Sarnoff said. "He'll have to be photogenic, wear the right necktie and smile pleasantly. But most of all, the candidate will have to reflect in the television screen whatever sincerity is in him. The public is quick to detect by the eye much that is lost by the ear." His prediction might have been ten years early, but in 1960 the election of John F. Kennedy was recognized as a true television phenomenon.

The RCA exhibit anchored the Museum for ten years, and in that time the exhibit was changed in many ways to keep up with swift developments. Most dramatically, in 1958 they converted the "See Yourself" display to "living color." If people were impressed by the small black-and-white screen, they were riveted by the color. This also represented an important opportunity for NBC, then battling CBS for acceptance of its own color television system. Several years before, CBS had been first to win FCC approval for its color technology, which required old-style spinning disks and a clumsy adapter for black-and-white sets if they were to receive any image at all from a color broadcast. NBC's "all-electronic" color was developed later, but it was more advanced and did not require the hated adapter. They were two incompatible systems. Exhibits like the one at the Museum of Science and Industry helped NBC push to its position as the leader in color television.

IT DID NOT TAKE LONG for the Museum to understand that it could do more than just explain television. It could use the medium for its own overall aims as well. The Museum's relationship with broadcasting, of course, went back well before commercial television. In the 1920s, radio stations were as hungry for programming as the Rosenwald Museum was needful of publicity. And even before the Museum opened in 1933, the listening public was accustomed to hearing curators talk about their plans.

With Lohr, the Museum's relationship with broadcasting grew more sophisticated, although there were times when the medium seemed to overshadow the message quite completely. For example, shortly after the former NBC president arrived at the Museum, he was asked to participate in a radio broadcast by "master mentalist" Joseph Dunninger, a popular performer who baffled audiences with feats of telepathy. In the program, Dunninger somehow identified words chosen from a page by subjects on the telephone a thousand miles away. He made other guesses that amazed and amused the audience. It was hard to land on any true scientific principle involved in Dunninger's act, but the Museum of Science and Industry was mentioned prominently, and that was an opportunity that Lohr, more impresario than arbiter, was never one to pass up.

A decade later, in the '50s, the Museum was equally successful at getting on television. Early forays on the small screen involved Dan MacMaster, by then the Museum's director, as host of a succession of quiz shows. One of these was a WGN-TV program called *It's a Curious Thing.* Similar to *What's My Line?* this show had MacMaster holding up an object from the Museum's collection and celebrity panelists making guesses as to what the object was.

It might be a rosin bag from a pitcher's mound or an apple peeler from an antique kitchen. The panel, with personalities such as Fran Allison (of the popular *Kukla, Fran and Ollie* program) and local performer Norman Ross, Jr., would then guess what the things were. Ross remembers that he never did get the hang of the show—he was too quick. MacMaster would hold up a cranberry picker, for example, and no sooner would the camera focus on the object than Ross would shout what it was. He forgot that a better answer might be, "A television antenna from a house in Skokie!" An object of this game show, Ross finally realized, was to fill time by showing how bewildered, if not zany, celebrities could be.

Broadcasting from the Museum itself began by the mid-1950s, when Chicago's educational television station, WTTW-TV, set up its small operation beneath the dome of the east wing of the building. The station built a studio with sealed windows looking in, and the television operation doubled as an exhibit, although most live broadcasts were made at night. The exhibit-studio inspired WTTW's long-lived tagline: "Your Window to the World."

It was a mutually beneficial relationship. Public television and the Museum shared an objective that had the relatively new name of "adult education." In 1956, WTTW inaugurated programs for viewers to earn junior college degrees by television. Several of the courses included broadcasts originating in Museum galleries. Atomic energy exhibits, of which there was a succession in the postwar period, were frequently included in the "TV College" curriculum. So was Swift & Company's *Food for Life* exhibit, with its lessons in nutrition. Staff members recalled that educational television truly came into its own one evening in this exhibit when the station trained cameras on the incubator filled with chicken eggs. Live television was never easy; in this case the director had to focus on the one egg that seemed most ready to hatch. He made his guess. The cameraman zoomed in. And within a couple of minutes— Eureka!—a baby chick was born.

While programming was often primitive, at least one classic bit of live television originated from the small studio. It was when Frank Lloyd Wright, in town for a conference at the Museum on the future of cities, was joined by Carl Sandburg for a broadcast interview in 1957. Wright was as ancient and ornery as ever. His friend Sandburg was as smooth as silk. Wright carried on predictably about real estate developers and their lack of taste and humanity. Sandburg, meanwhile, told stories of old Chicago, sprawling and brawling but still lovable. The show finally came to an end, but not before the two characters thought they were already off the air. "Come on Frank, let's get the hell out of here before one of us starts telling the truth," Sandburg said. Wright nodded with satisfaction.

IN THE DECADES that followed, television served the Museum in countless ways. The *Coal Mine* was televised on CBS in a production that might have been a presidential inauguration for the size and nervousness of the crew. Even *The Ed Sullivan Show* once originated from the Museum. If a television star was born at the Museum of Science and Industry, he was created a few years later out of a modest and unlikely character—Bruce Mitchell, son of a preacher and former law student. Mitchell started working at the Museum in 1957, quitting a career in business because he wanted to be a demonstrator at the Museum of Science and Industry. He took to the task immediately, and as his knowledge about the Museum grew encyclopedic, he became assistant to the president in charge of exhibits. That was his organizational title, but he was eventually known throughout Chicago as the "How and Why Man." That was what he became in 1973, when Frazier Thomas, legendary WGN personality, tapped him to appear on *The Garfield Goose Show*. His job was to demonstrate fascinating things from the Museum of Science and Industry.

One of Mitchell's first segments was entitled "How Tick and Tock Keep Time." To prepare for his few minutes on the air, Mitchell took several time-pieces from the Museum collection. With his lucid and friendly speaking style, he explained how continuous movement and the shape of gears are responsible for accurate clocks and watches. Over the next several years, he continued to join Thomas every couple of weeks to explain other things that were commonplace but interesting and sometimes mysterious.

This was still live television. Thus there were good days and bad days. On another episode of *Garfield Goose*—which featured a puppet posing as "king of the world" and his happily deranged court—Mitchell demonstrated the modern new material being used on automobile dashboards. It absorbed shock so well, he said, that an egg dropped from five feet would land on it unharmed. Conscientious as always, Mitchell practiced this routine several times before airtime without mishap. Then on camera, it was not that he was nervous, but before tens of thousands of children the dropped egg landed at an angle, bounced off the dashboard material, and cracked on the studio floor.

Television continued to raise the Museum of Science and Industry's public profile, and Mitchell could hardly go out without being recognized. One morning he got an up-close look at the kind of excitement his broadcasts created. When a young visitor to the Museum saw the "How and Why Man" through the glass doors of the president's outer office, then directly beside the front door, the child burst in. His eyes were on stems. "Hey, you're on *Garfield Goose*, man!" he cried. Mitchell smiled and the boy ran out to tell his friends and see what other wonders the Museum had to offer.

TWELVE

Keeping Up with Progress

Throughout the 1950s, the predominant message of the Museum of Science and Industry was clear. It was that the steady advance of technology was both inevitable and good. Despite this conviction—along with the Museum's skilled showmanship—new developments came with much speed and a few unexpected turns. Science was changing the world. Viewpoints and opinions followed.

The Museum rarely entered deliberately into controversy. But as the nation struggled with complicated issues of science and technology, the Museum of Science and Industry became a protagonist on the side of continued progress. This was evident in a series of exhibits on nuclear energy beginning in 1948.

Nuclear science was a compelling new field. The use of the atomic bomb to end World War II had ushered in a new age and was accompanied by the specter of unimaginable consequences. When the Atomic Energy Commission (AEC) was created in 1946, one of its objectives was to assuage public fears about nuclear energy and emphasize its peaceful applications. For this reason, AEC authorities in Chicago, birthplace of the nuclear age, found it useful to establish ties with the popular Museum of Science and Industry. "Scientists saw what they were doing as so reasonable and so intelligent, that public support was only a matter of explaining nuclear science to the public," observed Dr. Jack Holl, historian of the AEC's Argonne National Laboratory near Chicago.

The question of *how* to explain, of course, was not so easily answered. In 1948, the fledgling Argonne Laboratory, located in DuPage County, sponsored an exhibit at the Museum called *Atomic Energy* which illustrated principles of nuclear energy in simple terms. One of its displays was a radiation-proof box with a 54-lb. piece of uranium ore inside, which visitors could raise with a lever. A label explained that the brick contained less than a half pound of the fissionable element, U-235, but still enough to heat the average Chicago home for 40 or 50 years.

Almost every successful exhibit at the Museum of Science and Industry can be remembered for at least one thing that was completely strange and unexpected. In *Atomic Energy* this honor belonged to "Hot Frogs," a small artificial pond filled with live frogs, several of which had been injected with a radioactive substance. From outside the tank visitors could manipulate a mechanical arm connected to a Geiger counter. When the sensor-equipped rod came within range of a radioactive frog, lights flashed and a buzzer sounded. "Hot Frogs," inconceivable today, suggested medical applications of nuclear science. Most importantly, it held the public's attention long enough to get across at least a basic idea of what nuclear isotopes might do.

A year later, Argonne scientists expanded the *Atomic Energy* exhibit and created something called the Atomic Energy Institute at the Museum. Over the next two years, some 300 math and science teachers attended Saturday morning classes at the institute where scientists explained the basics of atomic power. Here teachers learned that nuclear explosions are possible because the nuclei of atoms are packed together with a force greater than that of any other energy source on earth. By selecting elements with unstable nuclei, such as uranium, and accelerating the changes in those atoms that normally take place over hundreds of millions of years, scientists unleashed a new kind of power.

Selected students also attended events at the institute, hearing lectures and witnessing demonstrations. Some acquired real understanding of the issues involved. In 1950, the *Chicago Sun-Times* interviewed a number of these high-schoolers who said they were considering branches of nuclear science as careers. "I'm going into medicine and will specialize in the radiation field," said Morton Multach, a senior at Hyde Park High School. "Atomic energy is the property of the people, and it may be the means in the future of saving many lives as medical research goes on." This was good exposure for nuclear energy, even if some acknowledged its potential dangers. Robert Adler, of Austin High School, said, "I don't think there's much to worry about at present, but we mustn't overlook the fact that this business could develop into something that could destroy the whole earth. We need some kind of world control and I think they are heading in that direction."

While most were convinced that the nuclear future was safe, dissenting views occasionally found their way into the Museum. Not long after the Atomic Energy Institute was launched, another exhibit, *Hiroshima Relics*, opened. Prepared by the Department of Defense, the pictures depicted the aftermath of the atomic bomb using photos, movies, charts and other media to illustrate the extent of nuclear devastation. This dark side of nuclear power had previously been shown at a conference of the American Medical Association. Here, it opened adjacent to *Atomic Energy*, and whether or not this surprised the AEC, it definitely clashed with their primary message. *Hiroshima Relics* had a short run at the Museum.

By 1951, the atomic energy exhibits were expanded, now with the safety theme more prominent than ever. One addition at this time was the master-slave apparatus, a set of mechanical arms that could handle radioactive materials behind glass without risk. On a photo-opportunity day for introducing this and other devices, a photographer asked if the thing could strike a match and light a cigarette. It could and did, and the moment was immortalized in the *Chicago Tribune*.

ANOTHER SIGN OF THE NUCLEAR TIMES at the Museum was at the Centennial of Engineering conference which Lohr hosted in 1952. In several addresses given by attendees to that event, nuclear energy was a prominent subject. In his opening remarks, the president of the American Society of Civil Engineers, Carlton S. Proctor, expressed the view that the principal menace vis-à-vis nuclear energy was not unloosed radiation, but rather the Soviet Union. Still, Proctor was mystified by the advent of nuclear research in Russia. "The Russians have brilliant physicists and mathematicians, brilliant purely in theory," said Proctor. "In jet propulsion they are probably ahead of us in theory. But theory alone does not produce an A-bomb, or an army, or morale." His conclusion was that recent atomic "tests" in the Soviet Union were probably accidents. He added that advances in Soviet nuclear science probably resulted from information from spies, such as the recently prosecuted Julius and Ethel Rosenberg.

As the decade progressed, Argonne developed additional exhibits at the Museum. Increasingly, Argonne's objective was less to address nuclear fears than to promote various applications being developed by the nearby laboratory. Typical of nuclear exhibits by 1953 was a model of the new nuclear submarine, *Nautilus*, at the heart of which was a light water reactor, developed in part by Argonne scientists. For the Museum it was a perfect fit as well. By the following year, the *Nautilus* model captured the attention of many visitors who otherwise would have brushed by nuclear science on their way to see the *U-505*.

Although visitors to the Museum could not know it, some exhibits on nuclear energy grew out of disputes, sometimes contentious, among scientists over the proper course of atomic research. In 1956, for example, Argonne installed a new exhibit called *Atoms for Peace*, featuring a hall full of models of nuclear power reactors. Nuclear power generation, not weaponry, was the direction strongly and even clamorously promoted by many Argonne scientists, some of whom were involved in the antimilitary *Bulletin of the Atomic Scientists*.

The Museum of Science and Industry was not a stage for disputes of this

kind, but there were still other pressures beneath the surface. While many people, particularly at Argonne, insisted that public utilities could and must embark
on nuclear programs immediately, a faction of high-energy physicists connected
to the AEC disagreed, saying that the technology was not ready. *Atoms for Peace*
strongly advanced the case for nuclear energy; it also reflected the fact that
Argonne Lab was largely responsible for the technology which Chicago-based
Commonwealth Edison was soon to embrace wholeheartedly.

THE MUSEUM OF SCIENCE AND INDUSTRY became a stage for large
and well-funded organizations to tell their stories. Lohr's museum provided an
ideal audience—large, young and receptive to new ideas. In return, they spent
ample money for handsome installations and promised to maintain them with
updated information as it became available.

Among such exhibitors, the Chicago Heart Association opened *Here Is
Your Heart* in 1952. On the balcony near a number of older medical exhibits, the
heart association approached a public that understood the often dire consequences of heart disease, but not what they could do about it. Using the considerable talents of medical illustrators at the University of Illinois Medical
School, the human heart was portrayed as a knowable and controllable organ.
The most famous and enduring element of the exhibit was the walk-through
heart. Sixteen feet high, it allowed visitors to explore its inside, an experience
that was likened to visiting a primeval cave. It served as the entrance to an
exhibit that also had push buttons, flashing lights and an array of clever demonstrations.

Over the years, the heart exhibit changed as knowledge about heart disease increased. When the exhibit first opened, a question-and-answer panel
asked, "Is heart disease inherited?" Answer: "No. Only tendencies are inherited." Question: "Does overweight cause heart disease? Answer: "No. But overweight is an extra load which may help your heart to break down when other
strains become high." With the medical knowledge of the day, the best that doc-
tors could do to prevent heart attacks was advise a life of calm. With this in
mind, the heart association included in the exhibit a specially designed kitchen,
outfitted so homemakers could remain seated and keep movement to a mini-
mum in cooking and performing chores.

In 1959 the exhibit was revised to address new information, specifically
the effect of obesity on blood vessels and the heart. By 1961 a new question-
and-answer panel asked "Who is most likely to develop coronary disease?" The
answer included several "new" high-risk groups: the overweight, cigarette smok-
ers and people eating high-fat diets.

AT ITS BEST, THE MUSEUM OF SCIENCE AND INDUSTRY was a place
that was understandable by children without being childish. And from the

The exhibit *Here Is Your Heart* featured the giant walk-through heart
when it opened in 1952. The 16-ft. model became an "icon" of the
Museum because of its enormous size and the experience inside that
its creators likened to a visit to Mammoth Cave.

beginning, its organizers took its young visitors very seriously indeed. Thus,
the Museum was the natural host for the annual Student Science Fair, which
began in 1951. The fair was conceived by the Chicago High School Physics
Teachers Association, a dedicated group of educators who were alarmed by the
steady drop-off in science education in many schools at the time. It got started
on a shoestring, with the Board of Education offering $100 to help exhibit the
best science projects designed and constructed by high school students citywide.

The science fair grew into a huge popular success, and within a few years,
corporations and civic groups were contributing $20,000 a year to help stage the
event. Many of the projects featured at the fair demonstrated a sophisticated
grasp of science. In its first year, a pair of incipient engineers from Chicago's

115

Lane Technical High School, Robert Schneider and Kenneth Smuddle, built a truss-bridge model to demonstrate the principles of construction design and "the resolution and composition of forces," as the *Chicago Tribune* reported. A group from Senn High School built a homemade radio set with a schematic diagram on the chassis to explain how radio waves were translated into sound.

Early on, a few of the youngsters entering the science fair showed they could also take a page out of the Lohr manual of showmanship. The most amusing display in the early years of the fair was a row of 105 mousetraps, each one cocked with a piece of cork balanced on the mechanism. In this demonstration the first trap was sprung by hand, starting a chain reaction that almost instantaneously set off the other 104. The racket was an illustration of nuclear power, with each mousetrap representing an atom and each cork a neutron.

Over the years, student projects reflected broader trends in science. In 1959—this being the age of *Sputnik*—Frank Rundle of Calumet High School built a model satellite equipped with temperature and humidity gauges and a radio transmitter to send data in the form of coded beeps. Also impressive was a 36-inch-long rocket made by a pair of students from nearby Hyde Park High School. They explained that this was actually a model of a more sophisticated vehicle that they were having made at the machine shop at Illinois Institute of Technology. That one would be of nickel steel, and they were planning to launch it in Wisconsin with solid rocket propellant that they would get from the Army. It would reach an altitude of 77.9 miles, whereupon it would enter orbit around the earth. There is no evidence that things got that far.

Also in 1959, Gerald Holmquist of Fenger High School in Chicago was awarded a trip to the Youth Conference on the Atom in Atlantic City for his Wilson cloud chamber, a device constructed for the visual study of radiation. "I have not discovered anything new," the young man wrote in his report accompanying the project. "I have verified my book knowledge by the results observed." A succession of directors at the Museum of Science and Industry never stated the Museum's own mission more succinctly.

Nor could anyone describe the true nature of science better than another rather unlikely visitor to the student science fair in that same year. It was singer-dancer Maurice Chevalier, in Chicago to appear in the Empire Room at the Palmer House. Chevalier, who became a faithful friend of the Museum and returned many times, was amazed by the things he saw. As he wandered through the maze of student projects, he delighted the people, reporters among them, who followed. Science was like entertainment, he was convinced. "It is chemistry. A man or a woman has it or they don't. It is a unique quality. Quite rare. Thank God!"

Chevalier had it, of course. The kids had it. And the Museum of Science and Industry, which could turn "dull science" into a media event, proved once again that it was laden with the magic dust that put it near the top of any visitor's list of things to see in Chicago.

THIRTEEN

The Medium and the Message

I n the 1960s, the whole world was changing—socially, technologically and quite completely—at the Museum of Science and Industry.

The decade opened in the space age. The unmanned satellites *Sputnik* and *Explorer* had been launched in 1957 and 1958, and discoveries of the earth's radiation belts were prominent in the news. Soviet Cosmonaut Yuri Gagarin became the first man in space in 1961, followed shortly thereafter by Alan Shepard.

These historic events made the public hungry for science. They also raised the public's expectations of the Museum, and raised expectations were reflected in changes that took place in almost every aspect of the Museum of Science and Industry in the next several years.

Actually, the decade's first major change was inauspicious. In 1960, RCA made the shocking decision to remove its exhibit. Only two years before, color television had created one of Chicago's earliest Museum blockbusters. Now, with outer space and other high technologies rushing inexorably forward, the RCA exhibit's attendance dropped markedly. The decision was also tied to RCA's cash flow at the time. The company had just embarked on an expensive venture in what it believed was the next new wave: computers. RCA's departure was a loss for everyone involved. Dermott Dollar, the company's popular director of exhibitions, had tears in his eyes when he told the Museum staff. RCA was moving on. So would the Museum.

The prime space occupied by radio and television, just off the main rotunda, was taken over by Bell Telephone, which had been eager to expand its exhibit for some time. Bell Telephone and its parent AT&T had become, by the '60s, far more than the phone company. AT&T was one of the leading research organizations in the world, and it saw the Museum of Science and Industry as a perfect forum to tell a story that the public might otherwise take for granted. With instruments that were part familiar and part fantastic, Bell was equally suited to the purposes of the Museum.

Bell Telephone was not new here. Since the '30s it had been the exhibitor of *Oscar*, the famous dummy who began at A Century of Progress in 1933. Another early attraction of Bell was called the "Voice Mirror"; it was developed in the '50s. Visitors talked into a receiver, then heard their own words played back. Tape recorders were not common then, and this was a fascinating experience for many people. When Queen Elizabeth and Prince Philip of England visited the Museum in 1959, they spoke into the "Voice Mirror." The Queen picked up a receiver and slowly said, "This is how I sound when speaking with other people on the telephone." It played back, and she made a face. "Oh my, is that how I sound?" she asked. The Prince smiled nervously and nodded.

Oscar and the "Voice Mirror" remained popular, but Bell Telephone had bigger stories to tell. The company invested more than $2 million in the Hall of Communications in the '60s, and they never failed to impress the public with something new.

By 1963, satellite communications were a reality, and the company unveiled a demonstration of microwave technology. This diorama used miniature transmitting dishes and a tiny satellite to redirect a real television signal. Blinking lights showed its path, and the picture being transmitted was shown on several nearby monitors. Elsewhere, phone receivers were everywhere, and at each turn visitors could pick up a phone, push a button and hear concise explanations—of undersea cables, switching stations, even the mass production of telephone equipment. For the Museum, this was an early advance in the development of interactive exhibitry.

Bell's Hall of Communications became the most popular exhibit in the Museum, and in the next few years it was updated constantly. To its credit, the company was never shy about projecting itself into the future, and among its most exciting introductions was "Picturephone." This was something that was promised to be in every household soon—a phone that transmitted not just a voice but the speaker's television image as well. The product was definitely in an early stage, and Bell Laboratories was reluctant to release it for the Museum. They were overruled. Tens of thousands of happy phone customers walked through the Hall of Communications every month, and what Bell's director of public relations, Ernie Zichal, wanted for his exhibits in those days, he got.

"PICTUREPHONE" WAS PUT in a sleek plastic case and mounted on modern plexiglas stands. A hookup was made with two similar displays, at Disneyland in California and at the Franklin Institute in Philadelphia, and it quickly

Queen Elizabeth of Great Britain visited Chicago in 1959, and the Museum of Science and Industry was an important stop on her itinerary. Here in the Hall of Communications, with her husband Prince Philip and Museum president Lenox Lohr, the Queen is amused by the "Voice Mirror" which played back a recording of her own voice in the receiver.

achieved what it was intended to. It amazed people and riveted their attention—at least for a while. Visitors lined up to take their turns talking to strangers in the East and West. Conversations admittedly ran thin from time to time, but even then the demonstrators in charge were up to the task. On several occasions when interest flagged, they walked over to *Food For Life*, an exhibit which often had farm animals. They would pick up a chicken or a small pig and carry it up to the telephone. People on the other end were flabbergasted, and everyone was amused.

MORE THAN EVER BEFORE—more than Julius Rosenwald ever imagined—the Museum of Science and Industry became a push-button world. The Hall of Communications and many other exhibits of the 1960s constituted true electronic playgrounds, and testified, among other things, to the ideas of media

In the Hall of Communications in the early 1960s, "Picturephone" pro-
vided a glimpse into the future of telephone technology. Here, a pair of
Girl Scouts tries it out, watched by Illinois Bell vice president Charles L.
Brown (left) and the Museum's Lenox Lohr.

maven Marshall McLuhan: The medium was the message. Motion, noise and
interaction were the route to the popular imagination. "The Museum became
kinetic and more active than ever in those years," said Dan MacMaster. "That
was what we wanted—something as different from the traditional school experience as we could muster."

At its very best, the Museum of Science and Industry was not only about
the wonder of technology but about the intelligence of the human beings who
interacted with it. There was concern, of course, that visitors might lose their
focus in a place of so much apparent fun. The *Chicago Tribune* wrote in an edi-

torial at the time: "The countless objects the visitor can set in motion in the Jackson Park museum may keep an overstimulated mind skittering from one well-baited attention trap to another. . . . But if we have the self-discipline to apply ourselves to the details, or the concentration to give awe and wonder a chance to make themselves felt before we rush along to the next push button, we can have memorable moments at this showcase of our time." The Museum worked hard to remain true to a tenet that Waldemar Kaempffert articulated in 1929, when the Museum was in its ambitious planning phases: "Scientific principles and inventions are discovered and made to be utilized. What do they mean to our lives?"

BY THIS STANDARD, not every exhibit at the Museum of Science and Industry was a stirring success. But in 1961, with the opening of *Mathematica: A World of Numbers . . . and Beyond*, many people discovered that science really did speak a language they could understand. *Mathematica* appealed to adults and children alike. In some ways, it redefined the Museum experience for them all.

Sponsored by IBM Corporation, *Mathematica* was the work of Charles Eames, a well-known architect and designer who did not hesitate to think of himself in the broadest terms as a "visual communicator." As he worked on *Mathematica*—to open both in Chicago and at the California Museum of Science and Industry—he filled it with many colorful, even mesmerizing, demonstrations. With steel balls, blinking lights and many moving parts, the exhibit illustrated the fundamental principles of mathematics and did so to make the most casual visitor stop, look and perhaps learn. When Dan MacMaster saw *Mathematica*, he called Eames a "Renaissance man." The designer had used his skills as an artist, architect, historian and storyteller to do what the Museum had always tried to do—to give abstract ideas physical presence.

The range of Eames as a designer was amazingly wide. Early in his career, during World War II, he won renown for fabricating a molded plywood splint for wounded soldiers. Later, he adapted his plywood-molding technique for furniture that won awards at the Museum of Modern Art. He became famous for a series of chair designs—Eames chairs—and as they were mass-produced by Herman Miller, they became icons of the '50s and '60s. His style combined utility and beauty, a contribution that Eames believed was the great potential of modern technology.

This was curiously well suited to the purpose of IBM, which had long been aware that their products, too, would make profound changes in the way people lived and thought. As early as 1939, the corporation opened the IBM Gallery of Science and Art in New York. Shortly thereafter, IBM's president, Thomas Watson, Jr., began the IBM Design Program. This began with an industrial and graphic designer named Eliot Noyes, who worked on logos and interiors but also moved into product design; he designed the original Selectric typewriter, introduced in 1961.

Explaining the electronic age to the public quickly became a design problem for IBM as well. To solve it, Noyes introduced Watson to Eames, who began working on exhibits about this highly technical world. Eames found it to be a marvelous challenge. "One of the best kept secrets is how unpompous scientists are at their science, and the amount of honest fun that for them is a part of it," he wrote. When he was given the job to design what became *Mathematica*, he saw as his task getting across that sense of fun.

It meant getting down to basics. "Queen of the Sciences" is how Eames described mathematics in a small booklet that accompanied the exhibit. "It forms the base of many practical sciences such as physics, chemistry, geology and meteorology. It provides the foundation for cultural arts such as music, art and architecture." In numbers, Eames even found a way to think about designs of nature—a nautilus shell, a veined leaf, an egg. Mathematical laws governed them. What were they?

Strict answers were not the objective of *Mathematica*—instead it was curiosity and wonder. In a device shaped like a wide funnel, the elliptical motion of small steel balls demonstrated "celestial mechanics," or the way the planets orbit the sun as it was discovered by mathematicians. A "Probability Machine" dropped thousands of plastic balls through a maze of steel pegs to graphically illustrate a bell curve and the laws of distribution. A giant Möbius strip had an arrow zipping around its surface to illustrate the sometimes strange behavior of planes and topology.

As *Mathematica* was installed, some exhibits people at the Museum were not encouraged. It was too complicated, they told Eames. The concepts would lose people. Not only that but the exhibit lacked a beginning and an end—it would force visitors to wander. To Eames, wandering was precisely the point. There was not a strict sequence. Instead there were choices. As his staff later described *Mathematica*, some compared it to the designer's fascination with the circus. Eames loved the circus, often photographed it and once wrote that it was "a nomadic society which is very rich and colorful but which shows apparent license on the surface. . . . Everything in the circus is pushing the possible beyond the limit. . . . Yet, within this apparent free-wheeling license, we find a discipline which is almost unbelievable."

Mathematica's freewheeling nature continued to rankle traditionalists at the Museum. Indeed, not every idea in the exhibit came through loud and clear. Nevertheless, the exhibit was a smashing success. It prompted letters from people of all ages and at all levels of knowledge. A high school sophomore from Connecticut wrote to ask for instructions to construct his own probability machine as part of a school math project. A teacher from Park Ridge wrote to comment on the celestial mechanics device. "Members of my calculus class have asked me what the mathematical equation of such a surface might be," he wrote. "If it is not too much trouble, we'd like a reference to study the question further."

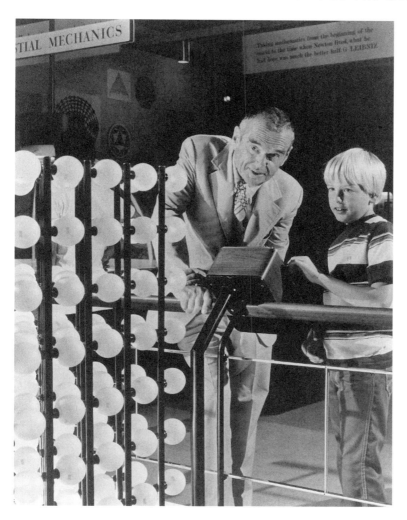

Designer Charles Eames discovered new ways to fascinate the public
in the IBM-sponsored exhibit, *Mathematica: The World of Numbers . . . and
Beyond*. Some years after the exhibit opened in 1961, Eames was on hand
to show a visitor how multiplication can be illustrated three-dimensionally.

MAJOR LOHR'S LONG TENURE at the Museum came to an end later in
the decade. The last new exhibit he witnessed at the Museum concerned a more
prosaic subject; on May 28, 1968, Standard Oil of Indiana was honored at a
dinner to open the company's new Petroleum Hall. It was a typical Lohr
event, with Standard senior management at the head table and dignitaries in
the audience. As festivities began that evening, the Museum's director, Daniel
MacMaster introduced the Major, whose remarks were strangely brief.

Lohr then yielded the podium to the executives and to Senator Charles Percy, who was also attending that night. While the others spoke, Lohr quietly got up and walked to the president's office which was beside the main entrance. He was followed by his wife and his executive assistant, Janet Irwin.

People who knew Lohr had their eye on him, because he had been in poor health for some time. A few minutes later they saw him come out of his office in his coat. He was obviously feeling ill, but not so ill that he failed to glance back at the people seated in the North Court. One of them remembered that Lohr looked straight at her, smiled weakly, and waved. Then he left. Mrs. Lohr and Miss Irwin were to drive the Major home and put him to bed.

They never made it. Before their car turned onto Lake Shore Drive, Lenox Lohr suffered what was later determined to be cardiac arrest. By the time they got him to the emergency room at the University of Chicago Hospital, only a mile away, he was dead at the age of 77. From the hospital, Janet Irwin was able to call MacMaster at the Museum. Before the night was over, the director called several trustees to tell them that an era at the Museum had come to a close.

WHEN THE TRUSTEES MADE Dan MacMaster president of the Museum of Science and Industry a week later, the transition was anything but turbulent. MacMaster knew the Museum as well as anyone could, having been on the curatorial staff since 1933 when his then-employer T. E. Donnelley of the printing company R.R. Donnelley & Sons Company "loaned" him to the Museum (Donnelley was a trustee) to oversee the printing exhibit.

MacMaster was a survivor of the curatorial purge in 1940 and soon became the Major's right-hand man. Made director in 1950 at the age of 37, he was Lohr's heir apparent, and by the 1960s he was managing day-to-day affairs, steering the Museum through a difficult decade. MacMaster oversaw changes which took place almost monthly in the exhibit halls—technology was advancing swiftly and the Museum grew in popularity. He also took charge as other events unfolded less by design than as symptoms of troubled times. Leadership through these waters required more than a modicum of diplomacy, which was one of MacMaster's strengths.

Exhibits about the Soviet Union came to the Museum in this period, and they were frequently interesting for the most unpredictable reasons. It was the time of the Cold War—the Bay of Pigs took place in 1961, and in 1962 Kennedy faced down Khrushchev in the Cuban Missile Crisis. Nevertheless, as both sides searched for common bonds, they often found them in cultural exchanges. For these, the Museum of Science and Industry was a likely venue.

These exchange programs were frequently successful, but from time to time they resulted in strange and even comic encounters. One of the first such exhibits was the *Soviet Exposition of Medicine and Medical Equipment* in 1961. It was meant to be mild and uncontroversial, and relations between the Russians and Americans assigned to install the exhibit at the Museum of Science and Industry were good. It was because of these good relations, in fact, that MacMaster's exhibits manager, Olaf Harringer, was concerned when he saw what was going into a display on Soviet dentistry. Labels in English claimed that this was the proud result of decades of research. In reality, the equipment looked fifty years behind what was common in the United States, and it presented a definite problem. Harringer was reluctant to offend the Russians. But he didn't want them to embarrass themselves or the Museum with dental equipment that looked more like strange instruments of torture.

Harringer's solution to the problem was a study in tactfulness. He asked the Russians to lunch. They went to a nearby restaurant, and afterward they stopped in at a dentist's office in the Hyde Park Bank building. The Russians were wide-eyed as they toured the small office. The chair and console looked positively space-age to them. Back at the Museum they had a short conference among themselves, then came to Harringer. They had decided to put the dentist's equipment back in its crates.

Other stories of Russians in the Museum illustrate the tense, sometimes madcap, tenor of the times. In 1963, an exhibit of Soviet technical books was a strange hit at the Museum. The subject was moderately boring, but the Cold War made live Russians themselves an exotic and irresistible attraction. Added to this were demonstrations by local Polish and Baltic-nation groups outside in the parking lot. Again, relations were friendly inside the Museum, but this time the U.S. State Department seemed particularly nervous. U.S.-Soviet tensions were running higher than usual at the time. Then one day, halfway through the monthlong exhibit, a U.S. government official asked for an emergency meeting with Dan MacMaster.

The official explained what had become a sticky situation. As part of the agreement that brought the exhibit to Chicago, a similar exhibit of American books was currently on display in Moscow, where inexplicably the Russians had locked the American delegation out of their private restroom. The United States had no choice but to retaliate. So the Soviets' bathroom was bolted, and the visitors had to use the public facility elsewhere. The Communists took it in stride, fortunately, as this was apparently not the first time something like this had happened.

HOSTING SOVIET EXHIBITS often reinforced what the Museum of Science and Industry had consistently taught for the past decade: that American technology was supreme and in harmony with the Free World. But as the '60s progressed, cracks were marring the gentle gloss of postwar America. Several events at the Museum brought to mind Waldemar Kaempffert's assertion four decades before that technology and society were deeply connected. By the late '60s, the Vietnam War forced a reexamination of American society on every level.

The Museum of Science and Industry and its celebration of machines were no exception.

What did not change through that decade was the steady improvement of exhibit techniques in the Museum. In 1965, for example, the U.S. Army installed a colorful new exhibit, making use of a number of interactive devices to demonstrate the latest technologies used by the armed forces. The exhibit included parts of a language laboratory. It also demonstrated how counterinsurgency forces could pinpoint the location of enemy guerrilla forces on a map. Perhaps the most popular attraction was a shooting gallery. Visitors could pick up weapons then being used in Vietnam and fire at electronic targets.

Politically, 1965 was a tame year, and the army exhibit drew little flak. But in 1968, the Army revamped the exhibit to include a full-sized section of a Huey helicopter, the kind of chopper then in heavy use in Vietnam. The Huey was equipped with a machine gun pointed out the helicopter door, beyond which was a diorama of a peasant village. People could get behind it, aim at a thatched hut, and with an electronic trigger score a hit—presumably on the Viet Cong hiding inside.

It was no real surprise that protesters gravitated quickly to the exhibit. The Chicago Police Department had warned MacMaster that trouble could be expected. What was a surprise was the intensity of the protests. When the Army exhibit opened in February 1968, marchers appeared almost immediately outside the Museum. They carried signs and chanted. Some tried to enter but were discouraged by dozens of uniformed police officers stationed just inside.

Clever protesters did find their way in, walking through the doors like average visitors. Then at an appointed time they congregated beside the helicopter and sat down, not to be moved. Serious sit-ins were conducted at least three times in the winter and spring of 1968. Museum personnel would get on the bullhorn, asking the protesters to disperse. Each of three warnings was sterner than the one before it, and then the police came in and made arrests.

The altercations that ensued were unpleasant. So was the publicity. In May, *Time* magazine ran a photograph of the demonstrators with Museum personnel and police. As MacMaster and other Museum executives discussed the situation—as they did at their daily luncheon meetings—they admitted that politics was more than ever a part of technology. The helicopter came out. But this was only a harbinger of things to come. Philosophical issues that accompanied exhibits at the Museum of Science and Industry would become increasingly difficult—and increasingly interesting—as society continued on its swift and sometimes maddening course.

FOURTEEN

The Space Race

The space race passed through Chicago on April 9, 1963, with the visit of Marine Lieutenant Colonel John H. Glenn, Jr. Glenn was in town to dedicate the Museum's *America in Space* exhibit, which included models, photos and other objects, many of them courtesy of the National Aeronautics and Space Administration (NASA). It was part of Chicago Space Month, designed to promote space-related industries in the area.

Not surprisingly, the business of the day was overshadowed by the sheer excitement of a visit by a true American hero. After arriving, Glenn was escorted around the city by leading citizens, and later he came to the Museum, where a dinner was given in his honor in the Museum's North Court. Nearby was the exhibit with 18 models of American spacecraft, including *Mariner* (a recent visitor in the neighborhood of Venus) and a full-size replica of the *NIMBUS* weather satellite. Also on display was a mock-up of an F-1 liquid fuel rocket engine, whose original had enough thrust "to propel three million hot rod racing cars." The exhibit was impressive, but virtually came to life when Glenn got up to speak. Wherever the astronaut went that year, he drew large crowds as he beat the drum for America's space program.

In the afterglow of his 1962 orbital flight, Glenn reminded audiences that NASA meant more than communications and weather satellites. The future of America in space was in manned exploration, Glenn said, and he predicted that we would put men on the moon by the year 1970. Space was as important to us as the Western frontier had been in the days of Lewis and Clark, he said. "We'll need more astronauts, scientists, and astronomers in this space age. I urge the youth of our country to get the best education." With that, *America in Space* opened and became the Museum of Science and Industry's largest space exhibit to date. The space exhibits would only get bigger over time.

THE MUSEUM OF SCIENCE AND INDUSTRY had mounted exhibits on outer space in the past. Before the manned program began, however, there was often something unrealistic about them. Shortly after *Sputnik*, for example, when the Russians shocked the world with the first orbital satellite, the Museum hosted an exhibit sponsored by *Popular Science* magazine. It illustrated the likely future of America in space with models of what our orbiting satellites might look like. Most were no larger than basketballs equipped with rabbit-ear antennae, nor were they any more sophisticated.

The *Popular Science* exhibit might have been quickly forgotten except for one peculiar occurrence. Only a few weeks after it closed, the Soviet news agency Tass released an out-of-focus photograph that purported to be the famous *Sputnik* itself. No one had reason to doubt that the image was what the Russians said it was, but when Museum employees looked closely at the photo, at least one of them noticed that it wasn't *Sputnik* at all. It was a picture of one of the models in the exhibit and appeared to have been taken at the Museum. Word of this never went far, but it made the people who noticed the whopper smile knowingly about Soviet science, which seemed obsessed with secrecy.

The first NASA-sponsored exhibit came in 1961, shortly before the *Mercury* flights of Alan Shepard and Virgil Grissom. This was NASA's museum debut in this country. *Men in Space*, as it was called, featured a Scout rocket, seven stories high, just outside the main entrance of the Museum. Inside were models of *Explorer*, *Vanguard*, *Pioneer*, *Echo* and other unmanned satellites that America had launched in the previous few years.

This exhibit was not the hit that Museum officials had hoped for. Perhaps the uses of these satellites were too scientific or remote. Perhaps the title *Men in Space* was a misnomer, as the focus was on unmanned spacecraft. At any rate, it was clear that the public was having trouble crossing the bridge between science fiction and science fact.

In an effort to generate the excitement that outer space certainly deserved, the Museum brought in a scientist named Dr. Daniel Q. Posin as a kind of ambassador of the solar system. Posin was a frenetic and popular professor of physics at DePaul University, and it seemed there was nothing that the short, mustachioed immigrant from Soviet Turkestan could not reduce to compelling and entertaining terms. When he inaugurated a series of Saturday lectures at the Museum in 1961, he proved that space was not just important, it could be fun as well.

Posin was already familiar to many in Chicago. In the late '50s he was host of WTTW-TV's *Dr. Posin's Universe*, which began as part of TV College and eventually was one of educational television's most popular shows. Posin was famous

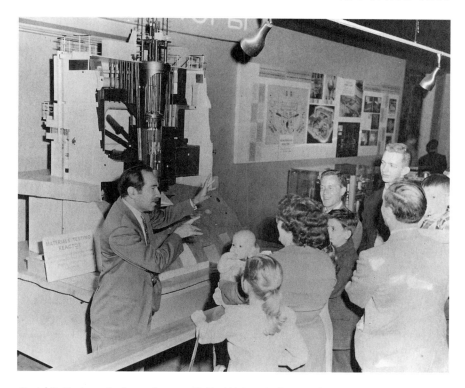

Daniel Q. Posin, a physics professor at DePaul University, became the Museum's most effective ambassador to the most difficult realms of science. He gave personality to the lessons of outer space and other branches of technology. Here he describes nuclear power.

for gesticulating wildly as he described the laws of nature, with sound effects of the atom "brrrreaking!" and the neutron released with a "pssssst" sound. So renowned were his lectures that when he visited Princeton University on one occasion, he was asked to perform for Einstein himself; Einstein judged Posin's teaching methods "very good."

Posin's lectures at the Museum of Science and Industry focused on subjects that people of all ages could grasp and get excited about—the future of moon exploration, for example, military goals in space and the possibility of life beyond our solar system. The moon, of course, was on everyone's mind when Posin gave his first lecture and provided many new angles on our closest neighbor. "The moon is one of the most fascinating bodies in our sun's family," he said. "It has no atmosphere, no water, no vegetation." Visiting the moon would be fascinating, he said, because it would reveal something of what the earth was like in its most primitive state. He predicted that such a visit would occur in three years' time, though he was worried that the Russians would get there first.

The lecturer went on to introduce concepts totally foreign to his mostly young audience. He talked about "panspermia," an old idea that the spores of life might travel through space from one heavenly body to another as a result of planetary explosions, waiting for proper conditions to grow into complex organisms. Often wearing loud sports clothes, always dancing around his blackboard, he would talk about the possibility (however slight) of turtles on Venus, which some astronomers believed might have an atmosphere, though it was shrouded in mist.

This campaign to popularize space was a tremendous success. As many as 700 normally attended Posin's lectures in the West Pavilion auditorium. Most of the audience was made up of teenagers, but a few oldsters came as well, like 70-year-old Emil Julius, a retired printer who knew Posin's television shows and wanted to get what most adults never had—an understanding of modern science. Through these lectures, and also through a long series of *Chicago Tribune Sunday Magazine* articles, Dan Posin became one of the most recognizable faces in Chicago. So great was his knack for explaining science that WGN even made him TV weatherman for a while, though forecasting weather was a little tame for a scientist who called himself "a cautious daredevil" when it came to predicting the future. "I get carried away sometimes, but I never venture beyond the things that are possible according to the laws of physics." This made him a welcome addition at the Museum.

A FEW YEARS LATER—though it seemed like another age—daredevils of another sort made a triumphant visit to the Museum of Science and Industry. They were the astronauts of *Apollo 8* who circled the moon on Christmas Eve, 1968, the dramatic dress rehearsal for the first moon landing which took place the following year. *Apollo 8*, with astronauts James Lovell, Frank Borman and William Anders, enthralled the world and further heightened this nation's preoccupation with space. When the astronauts visited Chicago on January 14, 1969, they were greeted by Mayor Richard J. Daley and then enjoyed one of the city's most lavish welcomes ever.

After the astronauts landed at O'Hare Airport, their motorcade was given an old-fashioned ticker tape parade down LaSalle Street. In ceremonies downtown, they were praised by the mayor, the governor, a United States senator and other dignitaries. They received medals that made them honorary citizens of Chicago. Lovell recounted that when he was a youngster in Milwaukee, he used to travel to Chicago in search of chemicals to propel his model rockets. He was usually turned away, he joked, by executives who said they only sold potassium nitrate, sulphur and other necessities "by the carload." There was no turning Lovell away on this day.

Next stop for the astronauts was a trip to the Museum of Science and Industry, where a reception awaited Lovell and Anders and their wives (Borman was ill). As reporters followed closely on their heels, they were given

The *Apollo 8* capsule was placed on exhibit at the Museum of Science and Industry in 1971. Astronauts Frank Borman (center) and James Lovell (right), who flew the craft in the first-ever manned mission to orbit the moon, were interviewed at the Museum in 1978 by Walter Cronkite on the CBS *Evening News*, on the 10th anniversary of their historic mission.

brief tours of IBM's *Mathematica* and Bell Telephone's Hall of Communications. The astronauts reacted with "the excitement of a pack of Boy Scouts," the *Chicago Tribune* reported. They were then joined at a reception by many of Chicago's top scientists and educators.

This visit was quite a coup for the Museum. Although the world of technology was a natural destination for space explorers, the visit was the kind of thing that made other institutions jealous. There were rumblings that Chicago's Adler Planetarium and Field Museum were hoping for a visit as well. But the fact was that the Museum of Science and Industry was first on any official visitor's list of Chicago museums. This was not only because of its prestige and popularity; it was also because the mayor's director of special events, Colonel Jack Reilly, was making the itineraries.

Reilly was an old friend of the Museum, having worked for Lohr back in 1933 at A Century of Progress. He was one of those gregarious, well-connected people who moved easily among VIPs wherever he went. After serving in World War II, for example, he became military governor of Mannheim, West Germany.

Afterward, he joined Lohr in Chicago where he served as special events director for the Chicago Railroad Fair, primarily handling the constant succession of celebrity visits. When that was over, Reilly got his job with Mayor Daley's administration.

"Do us some good when you're down there," MacMaster told Reilly when he went to City Hall. Reilly always did. Queen Elizabeth's visit to Chicago in 1959 was probably the most glittering special event in the city's history, and her visit to the Museum of Science and Industry was right in the middle of the royal agenda. In many ways the visit of the *Apollo 8* astronauts was even more important to the Museum. It led to a lasting relationship between the astronauts, particularly Lovell, and the Museum.

The public's focus on space exploration also promised to keep the Museum of Science and Industry first in the affections of Chicago's museum goers. The *Apollo 11* moon landing in 1969 brought this excitement to a crescendo, and the historic mission was followed shortly afterward at the Museum with the Midwest premiere of rare film footage documenting the odyssey of astronauts Armstrong, Aldrin and Collins.

While the movie drew large crowds, still greater excitement came in October of that year when the *Apollo 11* moon rocks came to Chicago. Placed on a revolving table for only a three-day run at the Museum, the rocks brought unimagined crowds. Whereas rockets, space suits and photos had attracted the public in the past, these brownish clumps of mineral proved to be absolutely riveting. A little showmanship helped, of course. Bright light illuminated the nuggets inside a nitrogen-filled chamber. A red carpet led up to the viewing area, and a recording of President John F. Kennedy's promise of an American moon landing was played continuously. Over 40,000 people filed into the exhibit that weekend, waiting patiently in lines that flowed down the Museum steps and far out on the sidewalk.

This kind of popularity soon prompted an invitation from the Smithsonian, national custodian for NASA artifacts, to discuss a permanent display for the Museum of Science and Industry. Olaf Harringer, the Museum's exhibits manager, was dispatched to Washington, D.C., for this purpose. He was escorted to the Silver Hill, Maryland, hangar where historic capsules and other relics of the space program were mothballed. Harringer saw many spacecraft that day that were waiting for homes in museums around the country. Because of the Museum's connection with the *Apollo 8* crew, it was agreed that the capsule of Anders, Borman and Lovell should come to Chicago.

In 1971, *Apollo 8* became the centerpiece of a growing permanent space exhibit at the Museum of Science and Industry, but not without its share of difficulties. The capsule was too wide for the doors, so Harringer had to cut a hole in the roof of the East Pavilion to lower the capsule in. Once inside, it became a predictable blockbuster and demonstrated once again the Museum's commitment to the understanding of outer space.

The *Apollo 8* spacecraft quickly emerged as a popular exhibit at the Museum. It demonstrated the fascination that technology can hold for the public, and the power of artifacts to bring visitors closer to the experiences of scientists, engineers and explorers.

SPACE EXPLORATION PROVED to Dan MacMaster that technology was growing at increasing speed and that the rest of the Museum of Science and Industry must keep pace to remain Chicago's top attraction. The Museum's successful chronicling of the space race definitely raised the public's expectations, and suddenly many earthbound exhibits and older technologies in the galleries seemed mundane and out of date.

Peering into the future was not simple, but one addition that helped show the way was an annual event that started in the late 1960s. It was called *I. R. 100*, and was an exhibit of the past year's 100 most promising developments in industrial technology. Sponsored by *Industrial Research* magazine, the inventions put on display rarely matched anything of Edison or Marconi, but they enabled the Museum to keep up with what was new in many technical fields. In computing, early time-sharing systems were exhibited and explained. A variety of instruments for environmental safety were introduced. Also in the exhibit each year were inventions that looked good at the time but never made much impact. A dental sealant to suppress cavities was one such product that did not pan out. Likewise, a $1 million miniature submarine was featured in the 1976 show but rarely appeared anywhere thereafter.

I.R. 100 was always well attended, especially by people working in emerging industries, a rather new audience for the Museum. Another benefit of the event was that it introduced MacMaster to Victor Danilov, the publisher of *Industrial Research* and a former *Chicago Daily News* reporter. From the time they met, it was obvious that Danilov had a knack for the evolution of technology and ways of presenting it to the public. MacMaster quickly viewed him as someone who might be his successor. In 1971, he approached Danilov with the idea of becoming director, the Museum's second in command. It did not take long for Danilov to agree.

AS DANILOV ACCEPTED THE POSITION, he knew that the 1970s would be a time of sharp and sometimes difficult transition, both at the Museum and in society in general. Besides coping with new political movements, the United States faced an undeniable economic shift away from postwar prosperity. The recessions and inflation of the early '70s heralded a more frugal period for everyone, including the Museum of Science and Industry.

At the same time, the needs of education were greater, not less, and they were highlighted by the general population's undying ignorance of science. This ignorance was a continuing and frustrating problem for the Museum. As a place for entertainment, it always worked very well, but as an institution of education, most agreed that it did not succeed in teaching the complex principles of science to most visitors. Danilov quickly concluded that greater attention should be paid to the teaching of real science.

This idea was not new, of course. It went back to the early imaginings of the Museum by Rosenwald and Kaempffert. The problem, however, was not new either. Basic science was not the stuff that most corporations, which financed the bulk of the Museum's operations, would care to sponsor. Private companies naturally were interested in exhibiting the products they were producing. And as the public relations dollars of these companies grew ever scarcer, it became clear to Danilov that the Museum was going to have to find new sources of income.

The year 1978, when MacMaster retired and Danilov became president, marked a conscious turning point for the Museum of Science and Industry.

In 1977, the Museum planned its *Nobel Hall of Science* to honor the careers of great scientists. Museum president Daniel MacMaster (left) and director Victor Danilov (right) showed a model of the exhibit to several Nobel Prize winners, including (from left) Robert S. Mulliken, George W. Beadle, Ivar Giaever, John Bardeen and Charles B. Huggins.

Danilov was convinced that the Museum could free itself from what a growing number of critics of the Museum regarded as "rental fees" for Museum space. Shortly after taking the top post, he discussed this subject with a number of his trustees. Until this time, the board had constituted more an advisory panel than a corps of high-powered fund-raisers. "Could this change?" Danilov asked. Several trustees said they thought it could. The issue was then raised before the full board. The solution was that trustees and their companies would be asked not only for exhibits but for cash contributions. All but a single member of the board agreed that it was the right approach.

Fund-raising was successful almost immediately, and $2 million was quickly raised in corporate donations and in grants from foundations and wealthy individuals. Danilov's vision of a more independent Museum appeared to be attainable. Then, in 1981, Mrs. Jay (Cindy) Pritzker agreed to organize the first Columbian Ball, a formal gala to bring more powerful and monied people into the Museum. This party, which spilled out onto the South Portico, was a glittering affair; it was repeated each fall as a regular highlight of Chicago's social calendar. With the help of a socially powerful committee including Mrs. Bennett Archambault, Mrs. Neil Hartigan, Mrs. Walter Massey and others, the first Columbian Ball was a financial success, raising $250,000.

With this encouraging response and a 50th anniversary fast approaching, the Museum next launched a capital campaign larger than anything previously contemplated, even in the era of Rosenwald. As trustees planned the effort—their initial goal was $15 million—they devised a long shopping list of needs to present to potential donors. Because science education was a clear emphasis of Danilov, several projects of that kind were outlined. A science library was one such project. A distinguished-scientist lecture series was another, and that was eventually underwritten by Motorola.

A critical moment in this campaign came when members of the board contacted the Crown family, longtime benefactors of many institutions in Chicago and around the world. Early on, the Crowns said that they were prepared to contribute some $250,000 to the campaign. So it was with considerable optimism that Danilov met with Susan Crown, executive head of the family foundation, to discuss where such an amount would go. Initially their conversation went nowhere. None of the items on Danilov's agenda—tuck-pointing the exterior and a new restaurant among them—had the kind of profile that the family was looking for. They were nearly at loggerheads on the subject when Crown asked Danilov if the Museum had a wish list beyond its practical needs.

After thinking for a few moments, Danilov noted that the Museum had recently been designated by NASA as the official Midwest repository for space artifacts, although the Museum still lacked a facility to display them properly. A space pavilion of some kind was something that Danilov had imagined as part of future expansion. Crown fixed on this idea, and even though it was well beyond what she was planning to spend, she took it back to the family. In part because of the Crowns' major shareholding in General Dynamics, which was an important space-industry contractor, the response was enthusiastic.

Meanwhile, Danilov dusted off plans—drawn up some years before but subsequently shelved—for an Omnimax theater. First introduced at Expo '67 in Montreal, Omnimax (on a domed screen) and its sister IMAX (on an oversized flat screen) used an extra-large format to project enormous, realistic, almost three-dimensional motion pictures. An IMAX theater had helped make the National Air and Space Museum the most popular museum in the country. Others were following suit. Because of its size and clarity, the Omnimax picture was highly effective in presenting exotic and farflung topics. And since museums and expositions had been early venues, the first films for the format were naturally educational in nature, ranging from a piece called *Polar Life*, for Montreal Expo, to *Tiger Child*, a tender look at world cultures for Expo '70 in Osaka, Japan.

Omnimax grew more slowly than some people had expected. The theaters were expensive, costing $3 million and more, and had not been built in great numbers. Producers were therefore hesitant to spend the millions required for even a relatively short film. The commercial potential of Omnimax was finally demonstrated with a production entitled *To Fly* in the mid-'70s. In 27 minutes, it examined the history of flight from the earliest balloons to man's landing on the moon. It filled theaters wherever it was shown and by the early '80s had been seen by an astonishing 40 million people.

As Danilov continued to study Omnimax, he was encouraged. Such a theater could generate much-needed revenue for the Museum. It could also provide an anchor for a space center which the Crowns appeared increasingly willing to fund. Not everyone at the Museum was convinced, however. IMAX and Omnimax were successful in relatively small metropolitan markets, such as San Diego, at the Reuben H. Fleet Space Center, and St. Paul, at the Science Museum of Minnesota. It was less successful in larger cities. In Los Angeles and New York, for example, the cost of competing in a market with many other attractions proved to be more than those theaters were bringing in.

Nevertheless, the Museum determined that it could make an appropriate commitment to marketing Omnimax. Then, as the Crowns drew closer to agreeing to a major contribution, they were finally convinced when Henry Crown, the patriarch of the family, visited the Museum and witnessed the crowds of children that filled the place. A space center with large exhibit hall and magnificent theater matched Henry Crown's image of the Museum of Science and Industry. The family agreed to fund a significant portion of the project, which cost $12.25 million to complete.

There were other obstacles. Some community members were unhappy that the perfect symmetry of the old Fine Arts Building would be altered with a new wing and a fourth dome. Their objection was overcome, and the space center opened in 1986. Its first Omnimax film, *The Dream Is Alive*, became a 40-minute blockbuster. With footage shot by space shuttle astronauts themselves, it brought to earth the experience of outer space more realistically than ever before. It also captured a part of the public imagination that had been moved by the recent *Challenger* disaster. "America was beginning to take space for granted," said Steve Bishop, the first space center manager. "Now they wanted to understand the problems and the dangers." In a six-month run, *The Dream Is Alive* drew some 500,000 people to the Museum.

The theater turned out to be the perfect companion for other space exhibits, including the *Apollo 8* capsule and an authentic lunar module that had been used for training the first astronauts on the moon. It also became the Museum's gold mine. The Museum's second Omnimax film *Grand Canyon: The Hidden Secrets,* drew 600,000.

By the late '80s, the Museum of Science and Industry was comfortable

The Museum opened its Henry Crown Space Center Omnimax Theater in 1988 with the NASA-produced film, *The Dream Is Alive*. The enormous domed screen and many remarkable images filmed by Space Shuttle astronauts themselves made this movie a blockbuster debut for Omnimax technology in Chicago.

enough with Omnimax to embark on a project to produce and distribute its own big-screen film, *Antarctica*. This was an enormous challenge—to support and oversee documentary filmmaker John Weiley, an Australian, as he shot quiet footage of life on vast frozen ice sheets and other mesmerizing scenes, such as the water ballet of emperor penguins deep in underwater ice caves.

With the Museum as producer, *Antarctica* experts from around the world were consulted by phone and fax in a serious effort to make the script rigorously scientific, but also spare and elegant so the amazing pictures might carry the story. *Antarctica*, which premiered in 1991, captured "the peculiarly human combination of curiosity and courage that has marked Antarctica's story," as the narrator stated. This constituted a compelling theme for any institution dedicated to the epic of science. Ultimately, the Museum's production was not only an artistic success, it was profitable as well, as the film was distributed to Omnimax and IMAX theaters around the world.

Still, Omnimax reflected a persistent frustration at the Museum of Science and Industry. Once again, some claimed that entertainment was overshadowing education. True, this was entertainment on a higher level. Omnimax even provided a glimpse of the future of entertainment. But the Museum of Science and Industry in the 1980s was still searching for a formula to teach the elusive lessons of science and technology. As the nation faced the 21st century, and as science illiteracy remained a hard-core national issue, this question remained alive and would guide the Museum as it sought a direction for the '90s and beyond.

Buckminster Fuller's "Dymaxion Car," shown here in the Museum in 1972, was introduced to the world at A Century of Progress in Chicago in 1933. Streamlined and efficient, it could not overcome the unfavorable publicity of a fatal crash while still in its experimental stage.

To 1984 and Beyond

By the 1970s, interactive, hands-on science museums had spread throughout the United States and to other countries as well. Much of this growth was due to the example and success of the Museum of Science and Industry, which was drawing more than three million visitors annually.

In Portland, the Oregon Museum of Science and Industry took the participation of local industry to extremes in 1953 by constructing its building with labor and materials largely donated by companies, unions and individuals. In Boston, the century-old Museum of Science shifted its focus in the '60s and '70s from natural history to science and technology, much in the mold of Rosenwald and Lohr.

San Francisco's Exploratorium, founded in 1969 as an institution specifically for young people, made major breakthroughs in teaching the lessons of science in a highly personal way. The Exploratorium brought interactive exhibits to a new level with videos and other moving images and measured their effectiveness in transmitting information to youngsters. So successful were American "science centers," as museums of this kind were being called, that they attracted just under 15 million visitors in 1972. The following year, the Association of Science-Technology Centers was formed, with the Museum of Science and Industry taking a leading role, to exchange ideas and organize traveling exhibits.

Despite their success, science centers were also subject to frequent attacks from the traditional museum community. "The newest type of 'science museum' is not a museum at all," said a curator from the Smithsonian, who went on to observe, rather rancorously, that they did not usually examine history nor exhibit many rare artifacts—these being traditional functions of museums in Europe and America. Critics also wondered if their concentration on contemporary technology would not quickly make most exhibits obsolete.

There were other misgivings. A professor of the history of science and technology, George Bassala, of the University of Delaware, complained that many technology museums too often implied that "technical progress was to be equated with social progress." Bassala was not wrong; some exhibits at the Museum of Science and Industry were emphatically one-sided in praise of technology, and a few verged on bold-faced corporate promotion.

The general distrust of the corporate sector added fuel to the fire. "Technical Coney Island" and "scientific Disneyland" were among the epithets thrown at several museums at the time. When the Ontario Science Centre opened in 1969—with an expensive array of lasers, cyclotrons and spectrophotometers set up for easy comprehension—an observer declared that it was "certainly not a museum. . . . It contains a veritable chaos of science exhibits mixed with industrial and technological exhibits sponsored by corporations. There is an infinite number of buttons to push and cranks to turn. Interspersed among all of these are hot-dog stands and purveyors of soft ice cream in a claustrophobic maze of noncommunication."

Danilov heard the criticism. From the time he was made director in 1971, and then succeeded MacMaster as president in 1978, he worked to raise the reputation of the Museum of Science and Industry. Among his new objectives were plans to make it a more dynamic educational institution. This would involve greater coordination with classroom instruction in the public schools. It would also require "less financial dependence upon industry and wealthy benefactors," he wrote in 1975, and more access to public funds. He envisioned science centers as places that "will continue to change and to adapt to the new needs of society."

Large institutions move slowly, however, and the unkindest cut came in early 1979, when the Museum was singled out in a report issued by the Center for Science in the Public Interest, a Washington think tank. The author, a student on leave from Harvard Law School, was concerned with the proliferation of industrial propaganda in science museums. He took particular aim at the Museum of Science and Industry for "renting out floor space to corporations, their exhibits little more than advertising." General Motors and Commonwealth Edison were criticized for presenting one-sided views of their products and industries. The exhibit on nuclear power was chosen as a particularly egregious example.

This assault was prominently reported in the local press. Danilov responded by calling it "hogwash." The exhibits in question, he said, were "presenting important educational information on two important industries—nuclear energy and automobiles." Privately, however, the report was sharply frustrating because the Museum had already embarked on a number of exhibits designed to change direction in significant ways. These projects were small compared to the major corporate exhibit halls. But the purpose of the newer, sometimes temporary, exhibits was to examine some of the broad social and economic consequences of technology as well.

The Museum's more serious educational tack began as early as 1972 with an exhibit entitled *The Design Science of Buckminster Fuller.* Fuller was famous primarily for his invention of the geodesic dome, which he patented in 1948. The dome was based on calculations and conclusions that an array of partially flattened pyramids constituted an uncommonly strong and efficient structure. Fuller's design drew worldwide attention when it was used in the U.S. Pavilion at Montreal's Expo '67. It appealed to people who were concerned with the limits that were being placed on a now-fragile world economy. The Museum of Science and Industry exhibit showed that the geodesic dome was only one in a long line of Fuller innovations that addressed the need for conservation of resources.

Fuller was a natural for the Museum of Science and Industry because his career was a case study of an individual's fundamental faith in technology. Early in his life he vowed that his mission was to "discover the principles operative in the universe and turn them over to my fellow men." This translated into a career as a designer of structures and machines that were compatible with nature, but which often had him near poverty in his early years. Among many such breakthroughs was Fuller's Dymaxion House, an ultralightweight structure that was designed for quick construction, with a central mast and steel cables for support. It was efficient inside and out, with a shower that created mist and used only a quart of water per person per shower. Fuller's ideas were widely ridiculed by architects at first, but little by little they influenced a whole generation of modern dwellings.

Fuller the engineer and visionary was forever working to inspire young people to enter technical professions, and he sensed that the Museum of Science and Industry was a useful forum. When Danilov contacted him to consider an exhibit, he was entirely open to the idea—with the altogether characteristic caveat that it must cost as little as possible. Indeed, when the Fuller exhibit opened in the Museum's rotunda, it was the essence of economy. Displays were mounted on a "tensegrity" structure, as Fuller called a framing design he had devised that obeyed the principles of geometry to make it light, strong and easily movable. It also made the exhibit flexible and convenient to transport and reinstall at other museums after it closed in Chicago.

Fuller made a hit in Chicago, amazing people not only for his decades of work but also, at the age of 77, for his utter enthusiasm. One glimpse of the inventor came at the Museum's daily staff luncheon, an opportunity to invite any outside guests to meet informally with Museum employees. An old custom, such luncheons usually started with a guest saying a few words before everyone began eating. On this occasion, however, Fuller got up, began to talk and did not stop. Danilov, loath to interrupt, finally signaled everyone to start eating, which all did except for Fuller. He talked about the many things on his protean mind. He discussed the failure of formal education—he had himself dropped out of Harvard where academic life had paled in comparison to working with real machines. He described the frustrations he had encountered with his Dymaxion Car, introduced at A Century of Progress as the lightest and fastest thing on wheels, but which had collected too much bad press after a fatal crash.

Fuller also had ideas about the future of Chicago. He imagined a giant dome covering fifty square miles, and apartment houses on the lake with modules that could be plucked up easily and moved whenever the family that lived in one had to relocate. Fuller was talking about a brave new world, of course, and if he was not strictly accurate as a prophet, his ideas were the kind that could excite anyone about the technological future. Danilov could only wish there were more like him.

TO ACHIEVE HIS VISION FOR THE MUSEUM, Danilov needed to find a staff that understood it—people whose approach to technology might extend beyond the machines of the present day and into the future. To spearhead efforts into frankly fuzzier realms, Danilov was fortunate to find a chemist named Dr. David Ucko, then a professor at Antioch College in Ohio. Ucko was tenured at Antioch, but the college had fallen on times hard enough to make him consider a move. As he examined fields beyond college teaching he found an advertisement in a newsletter that interested him. It was for the new position of research coordinator at the Museum of Science and Industry. Duties were to hire and head a scientific staff that would develop a range of new exhibits. Museums had always fascinated Ucko, and this was apparent to Danilov, who hired him after a single interview in the summer of 1979.

When Ucko arrived, he was struck by many opportunities for the Museum, but first among them was the general need for improved science literacy. Ever since *Sputnik*, lip service had been paid to better education in science and technology. Our very democracy, many people were now saying, depended on citizens understanding the technological fundamentals of society. Unfortunately, science teaching had hit new lows, and any small advance in the classroom was usually overshadowed by rapid new developments that made the old lessons obsolete.

In papers Ucko wrote on the subject, he cited a survey showing that more than 63 percent of adults had absolutely no understanding of DNA, and a measurable percentage actually thought it was a poison. Many other critical subjects were equally unknown, and Ucko speculated that the growing interest in the occult "may be indicative of scientific illiteracy."

One of Ucko's first exhibits at the Museum was a new section of the

Grainger Hall of Science, where the lessons of basic science were demonstrated. "Inquiry," as it was called, examined not so much the impersonal laws of science as the people involved in it. Though he was relatively new to museums, Ucko was convinced that science passed over most people's heads because teachers rarely tied it to practical or human experiences. In one part of "Inquiry," visitors could sit down and experience discovery themselves. With the help of personal computers, visitors learned that mathematical equations, albeit complex ones, governed the natural shapes of seashells. The concept was entirely abstract until visitors were invited to sit down at a computer, work out such equations on their own and see what a resulting shell might look like on the screen.

Reaching visitors in a personal way was something that Ucko called "emotional access." Since Ucko believed that humor often opened doors, "Inquiry" also featured examples of scientific phraseology and offered tongue-in-cheek translations. For example, "It has long been known that . . ." really meant, "I haven't looked up the original reference." The implication was that people working in science were not really different from the rest of us. Or when a scientist wrote, "It is hoped that this work will stimulate further work in the field . . ." it really meant, "This paper isn't very good, but neither are any others in this miserable subject."

ANOTHER PROJECT THAT UCKO BEGAN shortly after arriving in Chicago was an exhibit that opened in 1983. *Technology: Chance or Choice?* had a critical eye in examining the role technology played in modern society. This was an old idea at the Museum, but it was the first time it was expressed so directly. Development of the exhibit began with the creation of the new position of "humanist in residence," funded by the Illinois Humanities Council. The idea was to go beyond the "nuts and bolts" of science and begin "focusing on the decision making in the development and use of technology," Ucko wrote in an article after the exhibit opened.

Technology: Chance or Choice? began by chronicling the recent history of society's relationship with machines. The timeline began in 1932 with the development of rockets, and the invention of nylon two years later. It went on to robots and artificial intelligence and described the changes that these inventions brought to the workplace. The exhibit also made use of irony, with film clips such as Charlie Chaplin overcome by the assembly line in *Modern Times,* and Dustin Hoffman's famous nonresponse in *The Graduate* when he was told that the future could be summed up in a single word: "Plastics!"

Ucko was intensely curious about the public response to these exhibits. Shortly after the opening of "Inquiry," for example, he commissioned a comprehensive survey to see how well people learned. The encouraging result was that over 80 percent of those asked could describe at least partially what the scientific process was all about. While such statistics were important, what was even more revealing in these surveys were the simple statements of people describing their experiences in the exhibit halls. "I know I learned something," said one. "But I probably won't know what for a while."

In *Technology: Chance or Choice?* visitor response was an integral part of the exhibit. At one computer station, visitors were invited to compare statements made by scientists of the past with their own views of science and society. Results were collected on a daily basis. On a typical day, Ucko found that 61 percent of the respondents agreed with the statement of Einstein that "Peace cannot be kept by force . . . only by understanding." Eleven percent concurred with the opinion of Edward Teller, scientist of the H-bomb: "Stability depends upon power." Increasingly, Ucko was getting a better understanding of his audience. It was populated, not unexpectedly, by humanists.

KNOWING THIS DID NOT MEAN that basic science and its social effects could be blended easily into Museum programs. This difficulty was apparent during a visit by Dr. Linus Pauling, who came to the Museum in 1983 as part of a distinguished lecturer series. While in Chicago, Pauling also appeared as a guest on the Museum-produced radio show *Science Alive,* hosted by Ucko. In their half-hour conversation, most of the time was consumed in explaining Pauling's important but esoteric discoveries about the behavior of molecules in blood, which led to his interest in proteins, vitamins and other discoveries of medicine. Only in the final minutes of the show was there time to discuss Pauling's equally famous work in world disarmament. (He had won both the Nobel Prize in chemistry and the Nobel Peace Prize.) "Scientists should not run the world," he said. "But scientists have the duty to explain the scientific aspect of problems in the modern world."

Ironically, it was not always the greatest scholars whose message came through most clearly. Another radio program from the early '80s, this one hosted by the Museum's Carl Friedenberg, featured Dr. J. Allen Hynek, a former Northwestern University professor who had founded the Center for UFO (alleged UFOs) Studies. For years Hynek kept records of sightings of unidentified flying objects and other unexplained airborne traffic around the world. Among Hynek's claims was that our government was far too reluctant to investigate the subject. Their secrecy was maintained, he suggested, because unexplained phenomena might cause unmanageable panic.

As Hynek explained his understanding of frequent reports of UFOs, he talked about things beyond our current understanding. "I tend to feel that the solution to the problem lies in other dimensions," Hynek said. He discounted the idea of a "cosmic Cape Canaveral" launching spaceships to visit our planet. Rather, he said, sightings may be "projections of thought forms" from afar. UFOs might yet force us to accept "the next change in our scientific paradigm, as significant perhaps as the Copernican revolution."

ANOTHER EFFORT BY DANILOV AND UCKO to reach people without a firm background in science came in 1985 with a temporary exhibit entitled *My Daughter, the Scientist*, organized as part of the Science Museum Exhibit Collaborative, another cooperative venture with seven other science centers around the country. *My Daughter, the Scientist* told the stories of women who had succeeded in science, featuring their accomplishments and describing the obstacles they overcame. The objective was to provide role models for young girls who might not otherwise consider scientific careers.

One of the scientists profiled in the exhibit was Dr. Jerre Levy, a biopsychologist at the University of Chicago. Levy was skeptical of the Museum project at first. "Role models?" she said. "I never had any role models." She told Ucko frankly that she had made her way with almost nothing in the way of female trailblazers.

Still, Levy's story had obvious valuable lessons. When Levy was a child, for example, her mother had enrolled her in a book club, and because she was a girl, everything they were sent was about parties and birthday cakes. Only when she was re-enrolled as a boy did she get the kind of books she wanted to read. Another hurdle came in high school in Alabama, when a counselor from the state education department came to interview her and other members of her class about their futures. "I want to be a scientist," Levy said.

"You can't," the counselor said. "You're a girl."

"Well, if that's the case, I might as well go out and kill myself," Levy replied without smiling. "That's because the only thing I ever wanted to be was a scientist and now you're telling me that I can't."

After a pause, the counselor admitted that a woman might be able to get into psychology. Levy quickly objected that she did not want to be a clinician, she wanted to get into research. Later she distinguished herself in college and got into graduate school. But after altercations with professors who suggested she go home and have children, Levy left her first doctoral program and searched hard before finding a sympathetic department at California Polytechnic Institute (where 27 of 450 graduate students were female). After getting her degree in 1969, she quickly became a leader in understanding the way the brain is organized into hemispheres and lobes and the physiological basis for moods, attention and other subjective states.

ANOTHER BREAKTHROUGH OF THE DANILOV years came with the annual *Black Creativity* program. *Black Creativity* demonstrated that connections with Chicago's ethnic communities were one of the Museum's most enduring features. In fact, its earliest black-oriented events had nothing to do with science or technology but were designed primarily to make contact with people who felt largely excluded from the major museums of Chicago.

Black Esthetics, an annual event inaugurated in 1970, later became
Black Creativity. Here, two students from Marshall High School participate
by making a banner to hang at a science exhibit for the program in 1976.

Black Creativity's predecessor, *Black Esthetics,* began in 1970 as a showcase of achievement in the fine arts and performing arts. It was remembered as
one of the first opportunities ever in Chicago to assemble painters, sculptors,
singers and other artists in a single place. *Black Esthetics* was organized
primarily by Earl Calloway, the arts critic of the *Chicago Defender.* Calloway
brought the program instant credibility when he got gospel singer Mahalia Jackson as part of the first year's program. In her Museum performance, Jackson
was accompanied by composer Robert Anderson.

Black Esthetics included an art gallery, though a few of Chicago's established African-American artists resisted the idea of an all-black exhibit. Others
found it to be good exposure, and perhaps more important, the annual event
bacame an outlet for grassroots art. Sculptor Douglas Williams, for example,
had enjoyed a modest reputation in Chicago when the first *Black Esthetics*
exhibit was mounted. He joined partly because it was a major museum and
partly as a way to help young artists. "A few of them didn't even know how to
hang a picture that year," he said.

In three or four years, the juried show grew more selective and gave some young artists the start they needed. An artist known as Mr. Imagination was one whose early submissions were rejected but who came back later—this time with original jewelry designs—and made the cut. It was the beginning of a hugely successful career, as Mr. Imagination's distinctive folk art style evolved and earned him major exhibits throughout the country.

By 1986, Danilov was determined to broaden *Black Esthetics* beyond art and music. Through contacts with leaders in Chicago's black community, the Museum that year identified a group of people who were still barely visible— African Americans making a mark in technical fields. This led to a seminar for high school students to discuss careers in science.

Among the speakers at the seminar was a young man named Joe Morgan, a senior nuclear reactor operator for Commonwealth Edison, whose remarks had particular resonance for the children that afternoon. Morgan called himself "Joe Average" and admitted that as a youngster he had never thought much about going into science or anything else. "I was very much concerned with fast cars," he said. "I wanted to be the elegant man. But then I realized I did not want to be all dressed up and have nowhere to go." That was when he started thinking about careers. He said he succeeded not by enormous intelligence. "The key was motivation and determination."

Black Creativity became a major winter event at the Museum of Science and Industry, not just with exhibits and special programs but with an annual affair that became one of the social events of the season in African-American Chicago. The first *Black Creativity* Gala featured music by members of the Duke Ellington Orchestra, which was a sign of how seriously the community took it. Meanwhile, the Museum did its part to develop exhibits that merited attention beyond a single constituency. *Black Achievers in Science*, organized for the first *Black Creativity* program, chronicled the lives of scientists who succeeded against the odds. It later traveled to 11 additional museums under the aegis of the Association of Science-Technology Centers.

Making room for everyone in Chicago became a high priority as the Museum introduced new programs in the 1970s and 1980s. An alliance with the large Hispanic population led to an event called the Pan American Festival, inaugurated in 1973. This too began as an artistic exhibit, lasting for a single day in October, during Hispanic Heritage Month. It was a modest affair, but the number of people that turned out even in the first year promised that it would get larger.

The event ultimately grew into a monthlong festival, with performers such as the colorful Mexican Folkloric Dance Company of Chicago and displays of arts and crafts. As it grew in size, it also grew in the number of groups wanting to participate, and by 1987 one consequence of growth was disagreements among performers, artists and other people who believed the programs should focus on science and education. The festival was discontinued that year, but it returned in 1988 with a new focus.

Ultimately, *Latino Horizons* (or *Horizontes Latinos*) featured more professional entertainment and a clearer focus on technology and careers. Exhibits on natural history in Mexico, urban ecology in the Spanish-speaking Bronx, and architecture in the nation of Colombia were among more serious aspects of the new festival. A connection between space and Latino students was made when Franklin Chang-Diaz, NASA's first Hispanic astronaut, spoke as part of the festival in 1989.

AS THE MUSEUM OF SCIENCE AND INDUSTRY continued to redefine itself, it was eager for all of Chicago to recognize the Museum as a vital and contemporary institution. That was the goal of the 50th anniversary celebration in 1983. A yearlong lineup of events, the anniversary featured a Distinguished Scientist Lecture Series, with some of the nation's most famous luminaries—including Marvin Minsky, a leader in the field of artificial intelligence; Charles Townes, coinventor of the laser; and Linus Pauling.

In July of that year, a Science Jubilee in Jackson Park adjacent to the Museum brought thousands of families to what seemed like the science fair of all science fairs. On display in tents and in the open air were classic and futuristic cars, home-built aircraft, even a Space Shuttle cockpit trainer. Hot air balloons rose above the lawn, where blacksmiths, papermakers, weavers and other old-time craftspeople were making and showing their wares.

The Jubilee reintroduced the Museum to people who might have lost touch. And those who wanted to get thoroughly reacquainted were invited to participate in something called the Mind Game, trying to solve riddles that led clever visitors to secret places in the exhibits.

Obscure clues for the Mind Game included: "If you stare hard enough, you'll clearly be confused," and, "Where are you going? You've gone too far." The Museum was no simple puzzle, the contest implied. Nor was the $10,000 in prizes a trivial matter.

By year's end, no one had solved the Mind Game puzzle completely. But some came close, and two of the best were awarded the prizes, $5,000 in gold coins and a $5,000 personal computer and software. Best of all, the Mind Game got enormous publicity all over the world, and it emphasized the fact that the Museum of Science and Industry could be intriguing not just to children but to very smart adults as well.

THE MUSEUM OF SCIENCE AND INDUSTRY was now tackling more complex subjects. Dramatic change was not noticeable in the great halls of the Museum, but smaller exhibits consistently took on social issues in connection with technical subjects. Another exhibit of the Danilov years was 1984 *and the 21st Century*, mounted in January 1984. It was inspired by George Orwell and his novel describing a totalitarian future. It touched on aspects of the Orwellian vision that might or might not occur, or already had. This exhibit was "one of

Beginning as the *Pan American Festival* in 1973, *Latino Horizons* has featured colorful ethnic performances as well as programs focused on education and careers. Shown here in 1989 are dancers from the Mexican Folkloric Dance Company of Chicago, a longtime participant in the yearly event.

our biggest challenges yet," Ucko said. "For the first time we were delving straight into the future."

More than most exhibits at this or any other museum, the 1984 exhibit dealt not with things but with ideas, many of which were contained in films like *Blade Runner* and *2001: A Space Odyssey.* Even clips of the movies fell short of the exhibit's real objective, however, which was to get visitors to think about the future as if they had a role in molding it. To help focus the exhibit, Ucko engaged British futurologist Nigel Calder as a consultant; to explain futurology, Calder used parts of a 1964 issue of his own magazine, *New Scientist,* in which he asked 100 leading thinkers about their expectations for the year 1984.

Rocket scientist Wernher von Braun, one of the better-known respon-

151

dents, had been convinced that we would have landed on Mars by 1984, or at least made passes close by. This prediction was off the mark, but computer scientist Maurice Wilkes had done considerably better 20 years before: "We shall see everywhere in shops and offices, laboratories and factories, keyboards looking very like typewriters, but connected to a computer." The computer theme naturally ran through much of the exhibit, and it was accompanied by a warning. That was the "threat of an all-powerful state" like the one in Orwell's novel, a state that would dedicate itself to tracking every aspect of its citizens' behavior. The exhibit listed government agencies that kept such files, "in the name of efficiency," and it counted the number of personal dossiers then in government hands: 3.5 billion. The conclusion was self-evident: "Americans are not safe from the dangers that Orwell forecast."

With pointed warnings on the future of the environment, genetic engineering and nuclear war as well, 1984 *and the 21st Century* jolted people who were accustomed to the Museum of Science and Industry of the past. It received a less than warm review by at least one woman who saw it. She quickly wrote a letter of complaint: "Your institution is one of the preeminent in the field and has been for some years. Certainly, we, the public, could have hoped you would do a show of this nature better. If you can't present some positive aspect of the future, who can?" In his reply, Danilov explained that the threatening message of the 1984 exhibit was not the Museum's alone. In a recent Harris poll, 23 percent of the people responding said that an Orwellian 1984 was "very near," and 40 percent said "somewhat near."

What Danilov did not write in his letter was something he must have thought himself. It was a quotation from the beginning of the exhibit that came from essayist E. B. White. "The future," White wrote, "seems to me not a unified dream but a mince pie, long in the baking, never quite done."

Although never quite done, Danilov was still pleased with the direction he had set on course for the Museum of Science and Industry. With the completion of the Henry Crown Space Center, he retired in 1986 to a life of writing and consulting in Colorado.

SIXTEEN

Toward the Year 2000

Aserious approach to science was what the Museum of Science and Industry needed. Thus, the man who became the leading candidate to succeed Victor Danilov was a working scientist, long involved in leading-edge technical research. Dr. James S. Kahn, a geophysicist from Lawrence Livermore National Laboratory in California, was also a seasoned administrator. These qualifications appealed to the search committee, but because he lacked museum experience, several people, including Kahn himself, wondered whether he was the right person to run one of the world's largest museums.

"I've never worked in a museum," Kahn told the executive recruiter who organized the search.

"The board thinks that's an advantage," said the recruiter. Whereupon Kahn agreed to fly to Chicago to meet the committee of trustees that would eventually hire him.

One member of the search committee was William Weiss, chairman of Illinois Bell. Weiss had been involved with the Museum since he arrived in Chicago in 1981, just as the company was putting in its new and updated exhibit *Omnicom*. The experience left him satisfied but concerned about the Museum's future. Though the new Bell exhibit was thoroughly modern, he could see that other parts of the Museum were out of date. "This inconsistency was frustrating to me and many of the trustees." The board quickly agreed that a new president ought to come from the ranks of professional scientists. A person actively engaged in science or technology, they hoped, might keep step with changes that should appear more quickly in exhibits.

There were other problems that the search committee faced. The Museum had a physical plant problem, from the plumbing throughout the building to the roof overhead, and there were not enough funds to repair it. This was stressed by another trustee, David Grainger, of the Chicago electronics firm W. W. Grainger. He appeared to be close to leaving the board because these basic problems were not being addressed. Grainger's dissatisfaction resonated with fellow board members, in part because he went back decades with the Museum. Grainger sometimes spoke of one of the earliest exhibits in the Museum, the flight simulator, and noted that it had helped inspire him to get a pilot's license. His family later funded the *Grainger Hall of Science*. Grainger now carved out a distinct role on the search committee. "I decided to be a burr under the saddle on the financial side."

Some trustees wondered if the job was too big for one person. But James Beré, chairman of Borg-Warner and head of the search committee, insisted that it was not. "Do we want an overseer or do we want a dynamic manager?" he asked. The committee agreed on the latter, but it was easier said than done. The search firm would have to go as far as California to find Kahn.

Kahn's first meeting with the search committee was a success, but by all accounts, it was not a typical job interview. Shortly after it began, the interviewee was asking most of the questions—about exhibits, educational programs and the inner workings of a museum he remembered from his days as a graduate student at the University of Chicago. The conversation changed course only after one of the trustees stopped him—he said Kahn was learning more about them than they about him. Everyone chuckled and then straightened in their chairs, and the interview followed a more customary tack.

What did Kahn think of the Museum? one of the trustees asked. Having recently wandered through exhibit halls on his own, the candidate replied that some things were obvious. Scientifically, many exhibits were outdated. At the same time Kahn was intrigued with the Museum's potential and explained that he personally shared one of the institution's longtime objectives. That was the advancement of something that remained a desperate need in American society: science education.

The search for a new president of the Museum of Science and Industry went on for months, and the search committee examined other candidates, one of whom was a famous astronaut. But among them all, Jack Kahn stood out. He worked in the trenches of leading-edge scientific research. He possessed dynamic management skills—12,000 people worked under him at Livermore. His manner, moreover, demonstrated enough impatience to suggest that change might come swiftly under his leadership.

Kahn told the trustees, for example, that the state of America's science classrooms was in worse shape than most people realized. In the 1960s and 1970s, classroom science education had dropped to so low a level that American universities awarded nearly half their advanced degrees in technical subjects to students who were foreign-born. While they were still young, American students were becoming turned off to science in epidemic proportions. The

Museum of Science and Industry might help reverse this trend, Kahn said. Science was not a dead subject. There were constant developments, many of them exciting and almost all of them accessible on some level for students who were motivated to learn.

In one of his early talks with trustees, Kahn mentioned molecular biology, and although only a few of them knew that field in depth, most of them understood that it was responsible for an entirely new industry: biotechnology. Kahn also mentioned the enormous field of communications. Advances included not just microscopic improvements in computer chips and semiconductors but also new types of electronic imaging that were revolutionizing everything from medicine to cartography and even music.

Very quickly Kahn had the trustees enthralled. Science on this level was fascinating, and the candidate convinced them that the Museum of Science and Industry could once again take a clear lead in getting its message across. It would not be simple, nor would it be inexpensive to keep up with new developments. But a museum run by a scientist, the trustees now believed, might capture the undeniable excitement of those fields.

"This Museum is a sleeping giant," Kahn told the search committee, and if this seemed audacious under the circumstances, the trustees could only agree that audacity was what the place needed. Kahn was chosen partly because he knew the nuts and bolts of scientific research, but the main reason was that he made the trustees think in terms as big as Rosenwald and Kaempffert had some 60 years before.

AS EVERYONE INVOLVED in hiring him knew, the Museum of Science and Industry was not a natural destination for Jack Kahn, though his career path had never been a traditional one. After he earned his doctorate from the University of Chicago in 1956, his career became remarkably diverse. He taught geology at the University of Rhode Island. A few years later he moved to Livermore's chemistry department where he worked in the refractory materials division, developing heat-resistant ceramics for high-temperature applications. Along the way he acquired expertise in a variety of associated fields: statistics, acoustics, explosive deformation of solids and others. "I was not bound by an obsession to do just one thing," he said. Even as a graduate student he was interested in breaking down "man-made boundaries between the disciplines."

Midway through his career, Kahn developed an interest in business management, triggered partly by a start-up venture that he and some of his colleagues had formed in 1970. Technically, this company developed and manufactured refractory materials that were useful in the electronics industry. For Kahn, the private sector also underlined the indispensable role of accounting and finance in the conduct of scientific activity. Unless scientists had business skills, science was destined to remain the most academic of undertakings.

In 1971, Kahn returned to Lawrence Livermore, where he immediately

Dr. James S. Kahn became president of the Museum in 1987 and quickly reinforced the institution's focus on science education. As in the past, interactive exhibits remained crucial in getting across important lessons about science and technology. Here, Dr. Kahn watches two school children take obvious pleasure in learning.

began his rise on a different career track, technical management. In addtion, he accepted assignments in labor relations and human resources and also attended a summer program in finance at the Columbia University Graduate School of Business. By the following year Kahn was associate director in charge of nuclear testing at Livermore. In 1980, he was appointed deputy director of the entire laboratory.

Kahn's experiences as an administrator greatly affected his outlook as a researcher. Like other scientists, Kahn continued in his search for innovations and new discoveries, but after several years of management responsibility, he saw these concepts in a different light. Experience showed Kahn that stunning technical advances were not constant. On the contrary, he believed that the landmark discoveries of the 20th century—in communications, aeronautics, high-energy physics and other areas—were made decades ago, and that the role of science today was to refine established technologies. Kahn was convinced, furthermore, that the success of such scientific endeavor depended upon sound management of scientific resources. This was where creative thinking was needed. "The current strategic opportunities lie not with technology but with addressing the institutions of the social and political arena," he said in a speech in 1983. "That's where the targets of opportunity for innovation are today."

At the Museum of Science and Industry, Kahn was presented with a chance to influence one of the biggest social arenas of all, education. He was inspired by this challenge, and as he got ready to assume his new position, he recalled his own museum visits as a boy growing up in Brooklyn. He had been dazzled by exhibits at New York's American Museum of Natural History. Its million-year-old fossils, he said, had played a definite role in his interest in geology and his career in geophysics. He was convinced that the Museum of Science and Industry could do the same thing for a new generation of young people and move them toward an array of technical fields. He moved to Chicago in June 1987 with the task of revamping an aging museum, but he saw his most exciting job as helping "define the educational strategy for the year 2000."

THE EXISTING MUSEUM STAFF approached Kahn's plan to transform the Museum with mixed emotions. Kahn promised enormous change but was the first to admit that the ultimate goal was still unclear. "Living with ambiguity" was an often-used phrase in the first two years of Kahn's tenure. "If you weren't comfortable with ambiguity, the place was no longer for you," said one senior staff member of that time. Many older staff members were not, and a number of them retired. This was much as Kahn intended it. Some flourished in an environment where job descriptions were in a constant state of flux. Others did not.

The distinguished past of the Museum of Science and Industry was anything but discarded during Kahn's leadership. Marvin Pinkert, a new staff member who did flourish, came with happy childhood memories of the Museum during the Lohr years. Pinkert grew up near Hyde Park, and the Museum was a kind of local playground for him. The *Coal Mine* and the *U-505* figured among his earliest memories. In time, as Pinkert became vice president of programs, he agreed with Kahn that nothing was more important than the sense of awe and wonder in exhibits that made the Museum famous.

Like Kahn, Pinkert arrived at the Museum as part of a circuitous career path. After college he went into the government foreign service, then education as an administrator at Brandeis University and Long Island University.

When he was ready to come home to the Midwest, he applied for a position at the University of Chicago, and it was during that interview that he mentioned in passing his early connection to the Museum. The interviewer told him casually of the new president and wholesale changes there, at which point, Pinkert remembered, "My main objective was to end this meeting and call someone at the Museum."

When Pinkert met Kahn, both talked of their early affection for the Museum, and Pinkert mentioned having worked there as an intern while at Northwestern University's business school. During his internship, Pinkert had completed a marketing study which, among other things, researched how visitors felt about sponsors. His conclusion was that the most aggressive corporate-sponsored exhibits were ineffective for sponsors as well as the Museum. This concurred with Kahn's belief that exhibits needed to be less commercial and more seriously scientific. Eventually, Pinkert would rise to be vice president of programs, responsible for developing, designing and updating exhibits throughout the Museum of Science and Industry.

AS KAHN ORIENTED HIMSELF in his new position, he found that the Museum had unique strengths. The talented scientific staff assembled by David Ucko was still in place, and in small steps they were changing the way exhibits were imagined and produced.

An exhibit that opened shortly after Kahn arrived represented a model for what was being done right, and in some ways for what was not. *Learning and Learning Disabilities: Explorations of the Human Brain* had been in the planning stages for nearly 15 years. Its history went back to the mid-1970s, when Chicago neurologist Dr. Louis Boshes contacted the Museum to suggest an exhibit on recent discoveries in the science of the brain. Danilov was interested, though financing was an obstacle. Initially the Museum went to the pharmaceutical companies for funding. They declined, saying that their public relations efforts were targeted at physicians and not the general public.

The project stalled but did not die. Boshes maintained his interest and helped designers imagine a walk-though brain, much like the walk-through heart installed a generation before. Such an exhibit could illustrate what was known about the brain's grand design and the structure of tiny neurons carrying electrical charges throughout the vast network. Still, the idea brought no new donors forward.

When Ucko arrived at the Museum in 1979, the brain project was languishing. Then, as the biochemist assembled a new science staff, the idea took on a new focus. It changed from a purely cellular approach to brain science and began looking at the higher orders of mental activity, such as counting, reading and remembering. These functions were largely mysterious to researchers at that time. Still, they seemed more approachable for the average Museum visi-

First Lady Barbara Bush attended the opening of the exhibit *Learning and Learning Disabilities: Explorations of the Human Brain* in 1989. Here, Mrs. Bush is joined by Dr. James S. Kahn, Museum president, as they watch one of the exhibit's many videos illustrating the deep mysteries of the brain's ability to learn.

tor than pure physiology. It fell to the science staff to find a way to develop an exhibit that might have two distinct parts. One involved the hard science of neurons and electrical currents. The other involved concepts of thinking and learning that touched everyone's daily life.

The brain project eventually turned on the intervention of two benefactors of the Museum of Science and Industry. The important moment came in the early '80s during a luncheon conversation between Cindy Pritzker, a longtime supporter of the Museum and a trustee, and Victor Danilov. Pritzker mentioned new work that was being done in the study of learning disabilities—she had two sons with dyslexia—and suggested that the Museum might consider an exhibit examining them. Danilov liked the idea and said that Ucko's staff had been working for some time on a new exhibit about the brain. Pritzker agreed to get involved in such a project, and within a few months she was joined by J. Ira Harris, another trustee of the Museum. Together they agreed to fund an exhibit that would examine the brain in the context of learning disabilities.

Progress was slow at first. Exhibit developers struggled with the problem of explaining both the physiology of the brain and the experiential aspects where learning took place. It was a frustrating task, and there were times when it was on the brink of being scrapped. Then in 1985, one of Ucko's science writers, Anne Hornickel, was assigned to take the brain project in hand and move it forward. Hornickel began by attending meetings of support groups dedicated to people with learning disabilities, where she was impressed most of all by their passionate desire to explain their difficulties to the world at large. As Hornickel listened to vivid and heart-rending stories, she came to believe that the best people to explain learning disabilities in the Museum might be these individuals themselves.

Learning and Learning Disabilities—which was honored with an award for excellence by the American Association of Museums—ultimately covered many aspects of the brain, from basic physiology to the processes of learning such as reading, remembering and counting. The climax of the exhibit, videos of testimonies about dyslexia and other disabilities, were eloquent and strikingly authentic. In one, a young boy looked bravely at the camera and began listing his difficulties. "My problems are letter recognition, short-term memory and . . ." he paused " . . . and I can't remember the third one."

The formal opening of the brain exhibit was attended by First Lady Barbara Bush, who dazzled the Museum staff and members of the press by overruling her staff and mixing with the crowd on hand for the ribbon cutting. More importantly, Mrs. Bush's lifelong interest in learning disabilities underlined what the exhibit also was designed to achieve—explaining to the general public that learning problems of individuals can be improved through better day-to-day understanding by society at large.

IT HAD BEEN PROVED on countless occasions that emotion was an essential element of most successful exhibits. A measure of emotion was equally important in the planning process that began with the Kahn presidency. Redefining the Museum of Science and Industry would mean going to the very core of the institution. From the outset, Kahn declared that he was always wary of half measures. For much of his career he had denounced efforts that he saw as "tactical" solutions to problems. He was fond of talking of "strategic innovation" and "re-examining established values."

Strategic initiatives were advanced, therefore, with a zeal unfamiliar to many of the Museum's veterans. A new mission statement was undertaken, drafted originally by Kahn himself, addressing the longtime role of the Museum of Science and Industry as a "nontraditional educational institution." Whereas some of Kahn's goals were predictable, others were not. "Participate in the formulation and implementation of a national science policy" was one point that seemed entirely new, and some staff members thought it was farfetched. Others liked it because it demonstrated the Museum's serious intent. Everyone agreed, however, that these discussions were valuable. "I had this vivid sense that almost no one knew what the previous mission statement was, or if there even was one," said Ted Ansbacher, director of education at that time.

To hammer out a planning document that was entitled "MSI 2000," the staff went on a series of retreats. Several of them were held in a former monastery in Lake Bluff, and the exchanges were wide-ranging. Everyone agreed that the Museum needed revitalization. Exhibits were tired—technology had simply passed many of them by. Older halls, moreover, had an undeniable commercial look that was frankly embarrassing. The sense of the staff was that the Museum did not meet its potential. The real question was what its potential might be.

Some answers came quickly. That winter, senior staff met frequently for lunch. What was the central goal of the Museum? they wondered out loud. Education was an obvious objective. Yet the Museum sometimes seemed more focused on entertainment. Ansbacher, a former physics professor, mused that this conflict was not a superficial one; it went back to the institution's roots. "When the Museum opened it was half world's fair and half museum," he said. "Museum," in fact, seemed to be a misnomer. "Science center" was more accurate. That was because demonstrations were the real strength of the institution, not historical collections.

The next obvious conclusion was that demonstrations needed to be entertaining to get visitors' attention. But to what extent? As staff members compared their Museum to other institutions, someone mentioned Disney's Epcot Center, enormously successful at the time as a showplace for technology. But Epcot was different, most agreed. It used educational techniques to entertain. The Museum of Science and Industry was the converse. It used entertainment to assist in its real goal, which was education.

MANY SUCH MEETINGS ended on a theoretical note, but it was obvious to many longtime members of the staff that new energy and a sense of purpose was pushing the Museum forward. Then came a less welcome jolt: A detailed review of the physical plant indicated that the Museum was in far worse shape than previously expected. The building leaked, which was not news, but a decent repair meant replacing the exterior of the domes and the copper roofs in their entirety. Other aspects of the building were in equally dire need. The exterior limestone was deteriorating badly after nearly 60 years. The plumbing needed attention. Air conditioning, which was spotty throughout the building, was now de rigueur in museums. Among other outdated features, the emergency electrical system looked like the laboratory of Dr. Frankenstein. As architects and engineers assessed the situation, they said that the price tag for a full renovation of the building would certainly run into the tens of millions of dollars.

The building's true state was viewed as a major emergency. Initially

trustees even broached the thought of leaving the old Fine Arts Building altogether. This idea was quickly dismissed, but meetings continued with staff, consultants and eventually investment bankers. The solution was to go into debt in
the form of revenue bonds, a huge step for a museum that had always stayed
afloat through large corporate donations. It was decided that the amount of the
debt should be $15 million in bonds issued by the Illinois Educational Facili-
ties Authority. And because the bonds would require a steady stream of income
to repay the loan over a period of time, the Museum of Science and Industry
faced its most difficult decision so far—to charge admission at the door.

A team from the Boston Consulting Group, high-powered management
consultants, was asked to evaluate this unprecedented step. The team confirmed
what the staff already suspected and ardently hoped. The pros of charging
admission outweighed the cons, and new revenues as high as $4 million a year
could be expected right away. Among the consultants' findings: Almost all major
museums in the United States charged admission averaging around five dollars. Visitors expected to pay. Some even arrived at the door of the Museum of
Science and Industry and were astonished that it was free. At the same time,
one free day each week, traditional at most large Chicago museums, would keep
the doors open to everyone who wanted to come. Free admission to student
groups would also ensure the Museum's longtime bonds with the schools.

When a five-dollar admission charge was instituted in June of 1991, there
was an immediate effect. The hordes of children that had filled the central courts
of the Museum every day abated. Attendance figures were immediately down,
from 4 million a year, which was always an estimate, to just over 2 million. And
work on the building began right away. Dissent from the decision was also
heard, mostly inside the Museum from older employees who believed that selling tickets was a breach of faith and would change the character of the Museum
of Science and Industry. In fact, Kahn was eager for such a change. To the new
president, the admission charge marked the transition away from purely corporate exhibits and toward a more independent institution of science.

THE ADMISSION CHARGE also created an urgent short-term goal. That was
to make a visit to the Museum worth the price of a ticket. How to achieve this,
naturally, was the most complicated question of all. Most people who had studied the Museum admitted there was an orientation problem: visitors were getting lost as they moved from exhibit to exhibit, with *Food for Life*, *Omnicom* and
Managing Urban Wastes all arranged without apparent logic. A new scheme was
obviously needed. People recalled Waldemar Kaempffert's efforts years earlier
to organize the Museum according to some internal order inherent in science.

"Change was a messy process," said Peter Anderson, Kahn's former vice
president of programs. It was also slow. Many members of the senior staff spent
time wondering how the laws of basic science—physics and chemistry—could

be organized among the technologies of medicine, petroleum and electricity. Others came forth with ideas for new exhibits. But how would they be prioritized? There were countless meetings on these subjects. Finally, Kahn showed a trace of impatience. "What about themes? he said. "Themes . . . Thematic zones!"

The term "thematic zones" stuck. This was one of many breakthroughs in the planning process in those years. The new Museum would be divided into large zones or divisions, which everyone agreed should feature oversized, impressive images designed to leave indelible memories. Just as the old *Coal Mine* and *U-505* were stuck forever in the collective memory of several generations—and these icons would certainly remain—the Museum of Science and Industry must continue to dazzle and awe the public with its sheer size and power.

The planning process invigorated many people at the Museum. It gave scientists a chance to work with marketers, and administrators to work with educators. Early on, a scheme of four thematic zones was proposed, including nature, machines, the human body and the human spirit (or the process of discovery). After much discussion, the four zones were enlarged to twelve, ranging from the human body to space exploration. These were boldly published in a new comprehensive plan, "MSI 2000."

By 1993, a master plan for building expansion was also devised, which called for the expansion of the Henry Crown Space Center and also a new wing to the west. Besides more room inside, the scheme provided for enhanced park land outside, notably by building an underground garage in front and restoring expansive green space outside the Museum's front steps. The garage alone, planned to open in 1997, was to cost $43 million, most of it to come from federal transportation funds, allocated after public hearings which indicated that the Museum continued to enjoy enormous public support and affection.

As the physical Museum was envisioned in clear terms, the soul of the institution remained in flux. Sometime after *MSI 2000* was published, the number of thematic zones was pared down from twelve to six. This demonstrated to everyone something that was obvious to anyone close to the Museum. It was that many decisions were fluid, and until the Museum had completely revamped itself—something that would happen no sooner than the year 2000—the only constant at the institution would be change itself.

The Museum's Transportation Zone, completed in 1994, was crowned with a real United 727. Inside, the jetliner was equipped with a learning laboratory and a number of interactive exhibits demonstrating the principles of lift, techniques of navigation and many other concepts critical to modern aviation.

SEVENTEEN

Designing the Future

Early steps toward change in the exhibits foreshadowed the kind of science that Jack Kahn was determined to bring to the Museum of Science and Industry. The first new exhibit conceived and executed in his presidency came in 1988 and focused on "one of the hottest topics in scientific circles," as Kahn himself put it. It was superconductivity.

Superconductivity was not a new technology. In 1911, a Dutch scientist had discovered that materials cooled to a temperature near absolute zero could conduct electricity with almost no energy loss due to resistance. Superconductivity suggested unheard-of power in devices of all kinds. The problem was the expense of achieving such low temperatures, a cost that far outweighed the economic advantages of electric motors and other equipment that might benefit from the technology.

Interest in superconductivity increased in the 1980s when IBM scientists in Europe developed a ceramic material that could superconduct at significantly higher temperatures than previously. As these temperatures were far cheaper to achieve, the discovery opened new possibilities for superconductivity. In 1986, the IBM team was awarded the Nobel Prize for physics, leading scientists, engineers and even journalists to predict that superconductivity might soon realize its commercial potential.

But not yet. Additional work was still necessary, now not in quest of earthshaking discoveries but rather to improve the details, such as better techniques to make coiling wire out of the specialized ceramic material. Scientists understood that progress now would come in small increments, in large laboratories and small ones. Thus in the mid-'80s, when Argonne National Laboratory undertook a leading role in superconductivity research, a significant portion of that work was in public relations. Argonne scientists gave lectures on the subject and put on demonstrations wherever they were invited—in schools, at chamber of commerce meetings and in a high-profile event on the verandah of the Department of Energy in Washington, D. C. In early 1988, when Kahn asked Argonne director Alan Schriesheim for assistance in staging an exhibit on superconductivity, the laboratory responded positively and quickly.

Superconductivity, as the exhibit was called, required close collaboration between the laboratory and the Museum. It opened after only a few months of planning—near-superconducting speed by Museum standards. "We weren't used to working that fast at the time," said Michael Boersma of the Museum's science staff. It was a small exhibit but a significant success in attracting youngsters and adults and in demonstrating a strange and unfamiliar power. On platforms in Rosenwald Court near the main entrance, demonstrators showed how liquid nitrogen could create the low temperatures needed to achieve superconductivity. Small but powerful electromagnets were activated that suspended objects in midair, looking something like magic.

Best of all, *Superconductivity* showed how the Museum could combine science with live experiments and also illustrate practical applications for the technological future. Most impressive was a video of an experimental rapid transit system in Japan, levitated over a monorail and showing formidable and not-entirely-futuristic potential. Such images were vivid and seemingly on the verge of reality, suggesting that the Museum's power was more than simply in explaining abstract technology. By exciting people's imaginations, Argonne and the Museum both hoped that an exhibit like this one might even accelerate the path of progress.

SUPERCONDUCTIVITY WAS ENCOURAGING, though most of the people involved acknowledged that the exhibit was small and the subject custom-made for the public. The design of a subsequent exhibit, perhaps the most ambitious ever attempted at the Museum of Science and Industry, represented a far more difficult project and demonstrated that introducing new technology to the public was daunting even for a museum that had been engaged in it for over 50 years. *IMAGING: The Tools of Science* eventually opened in 1993. In the three years prior to that, its developers encountered more than a modicum of frustration and doubt.

Computer imaging is the process of generating pictures of scientific and technical phenomena and seemed to be a natural topic for the Museum of Science and Industry. The original concept belonged to Professor Robert Beck, director of the Center for Imaging Science at the University of Chicago. Beck's proposal for an exhibit was based on the fact that a whole spectrum of sciences, from medicine to astronomy, employs digital technology to help researchers observe and measure often-invisible properties. "Although each imaging modality requires different hardware at the front end," Beck wrote, "the steps involved in all imaging processes are essentially the same: namely, image-data acquisition; image reconstruction and processing; and image compression, storage, retrieval, and transmission."

Beck was the kind of individual the Museum had always sought. His career had crossed a broad range of sciences, and his end product was something essentially comprehensible to many people and not just specialists. In recent years, Beck had become an expert in radio nucleotide imaging and remained on the cutting edge of nuclear medicine. Beyond that, however, he was always quick to adapt his expertise to fields as varied as astrophysics and archaeology, and he believed that imaging technology was well suited to bringing the abstract dimensions of these fields to the public.

Beck was naturally drawn to the Museum of Science and Industry and especially its objectives in the area of scientific literacy. "These computers will attract young people to science," Beck told Kahn when they met. Beck went on to describe the future of imaging, and how new generations of imaging computers might be designed specifically for teaching—to present lessons in any technical subject, measure a student's comprehension, then tailor new pictures to meet the needs of that student. "These machines will someday be like private tutors," Beck said.

Imaging became an enormously tempting idea, and Kahn assigned the project to Dr. Barry Aprison, a molecular biologist who had recently arrived at the Museum from postdoctoral work at Indiana University. To bring the subject down to manageable proportions, Aprison commissioned a popular science writer, Fred Ward, to imagine what an exhibit on the subject might look like. Ward, who had written recently on the subject in *National Geographic*, provided many concrete suggestions, but at the outset of his report he made a pair of observations that, upon reflection, made the project awe-inspiring at the very least.

"Scientific imaging empowers us to look inward at the infinite complexity of ourselves as a microcosm of the universe and outward toward infinity itself," Ward wrote. This led to the question: how can we fit the infinitesimal workings of the human body into an exhibit that also broaches the outer limits of astrophysics and astronomy? Another challenge was framed in a deceptively simple dichotomy: "First, the images themselves introduce new information about the scientific principles or the objects being shown," Ward explained. "Second, exhibit visitors learn how such amazing images are made." In other words, an exhibit on imaging science ought to provide information about the medium as well as the message of scientific imaging.

Money came to the project from the National Science Foundation and a variety of other sources. The plan was for the exhibit to take three years to complete and cost over $4 million. It might have seemed luxurious in terms of time and money. But when the first drawings for the exhibit came from outside designers, they fell quite flat. With one eye on Kahn's "MSI 2000" document, the designers were searching for an icon, something big and impressive to capture both the attention of the public and the essence of the subject. Their centerpiece, perhaps their icon, was a virtual-reality helicopter. Visitors would get in and enjoy a simulated ride over Chicago. They could look out over realistic landmarks of the city's topography. By pushing various buttons they might also witness invisible characteristics of the city—population density, heat emitted by buildings, even pollution in the lake and river.

When Kahn and Aprison saw this and other aspects of the scheme, they were bothered. The helicopter demonstrated what imaging science could do but did little to explain how it did it, and other ideas for the proposed exhibit had the same problem. After considerable thought, the two men concluded that the designers may have understood aspects of scientific imaging, but not the objectives of the Museum.

So Aprison assembled a new team of designers and computer experts. Now under considerable time pressure, this group began by asking themselves a fundamental question: What had made the Museum of Science and Industry successful in the past? One undeniable answer was interactive exhibits that showed not just what technology did but also how and sometimes why. They all realized, moreover, that the computers that made imaging science work were nothing if not interactive.

Ultimately, the successful formula for the imaging exhibit was a variety of exhibit stations, such as "Seeing Sound," with a microphone to pick up recorded music or the voice of a visitor, and instruments such as an oscilloscope and tonal pattern screen to display various characteristics of that sound. Another exhibit station was called "Morphing"; it created an image of the visitor's own face on a screen to be manipulated or distorted in entertaining ways.

These exhibits would look like machines and not toys. "Don't camouflage the technology," said an in-house designer in a meeting at a crucial moment in the project. It was good advice and was well-heeded. Other parts of the imaging exhibit had the distinct profile of high technology, with push buttons, cables, monitors and touch screens. The icon of the exhibit, a large and impressive section devoted to virtual reality, took visitors on a visual flight through the walls of the Museum and into Chicago and beyond. This version of virtual reality resembled not the inside of a helicopter, as previously proposed, but rather the interior of precisely what it was—a laboratory.

IMAGING: The Tools of Science was awarded a coveted Curators' Committee Award from the American Association of Museums in 1994. It was praised for its originality in getting complicated ideas across. It also was influential for other museums searching for ways to introduce new computer technologies. Most importantly, it underlined for the Museum itself that its most ambitious exhibit to date was successful because of things that the institution

As technology grows more complex, so do the tools that are used to explore and explain it. Here, youngsters use touch screens in the Museum's "Mystery Lab" where visitors employ computer imaging technologies to solve a fictional police investigation.

had done well from the beginning. It got people up close to real machines. It capitalized on the natural curiosity of people, including youngsters and non-technical people, about the way things work.

EVEN BEFORE *IMAGING: The Tools of Science* was opened, the Museum saw it as more than a conventional exhibit. Staff members believed it could help advance a cause that had eluded the institution for decades—a strong, sustained role in education. James Kahn had even named the concept: the "uncommon classroom." It referred to myriad opportunities for the Museum to promote the goals of education in real and measurable ways.

This objective had intrigued the Museum's founders even before they opened in 1933. As early as the late '20s, the Museum had made contact with educators at the highest level. Superintendent William J. Bogan of the Chicago public schools often corresponded with Julius Rosenwald, though the relationship between Museum and schools in the 1930s rarely went beyond occasional student field trips.

In the 1940s, the Museum continued to address the possibility that the

Museum could be used by the schools to augment and enhance classroom lessons. Much study was made of this concept, particularly at the University of Chicago's esteemed School of Education. Still, scholars recognized that the primary obstacle between the Museum and true education was the difference between entertainment, at which many museums excelled, and education, which normally required step-by-step discipline. This question went largely unanswered, and for decades the Museum of Science and Industry only infrequently succeeded in teaching sustained lessons.

By the 1980s, the nation's scientific literacy was portrayed as more dire with every passing year, and one of the first objectives Kahn set for himself when he arrived as president was to cultivate closer relations between the public schools and the Museum. In talks with staff and in interviews with the press, Kahn talked about the Museum as an "uncommon classroom." It meant many things—including the opportunity for parents and children to learn important lessons in an interactive and social environment. It also meant that the Museum and the schools could work in close harmony, with class groups visiting exhibits with more regularity and after focused preparation with their teachers.

In 1993, members of the Museum staff articulated such an education strategy in a major report. The "uncommon classroom," it stated, explained the conviction that much childhood and adolescent education takes place outside the strict confines of school. Related was the observation that learning is most powerful when students explore at their own pace, asking questions and satisfying curiosity. The report went on to observe that the Museum of Science and Industry was custom-made for self-discovery.

The educational strategy report also proposed a number of techniques and programs. Among them were learning laboratories which would become integral to all major new exhibits, where children might become familiar with a technology, grow curious about it and spend time in working toward answers connected to it.

A learning laboratory was quickly conceived as a part of the *Imaging* exhibit, which was natural because the machines that comprised it were designed precisely for the purpose of illustrating, and in many ways teaching. With the goal of capturing the attention of restless students, members of the education department joined the *Imaging* team to devise a realistic and exciting scenario that involved many of the machines introduced in the exhibit.

The team determined that a mystery might ignite curiosity. After many discussions about the subject, a script written primarily by Museum educator Kirsten Ellenbogen centered on a young woman who has lost consciousness in the Museum. After paramedics find a lottery ticket worth millions in her coat, and because the ticket is about to expire, it becomes a matter of extreme urgency to determine her identity. Students in the learning lab are enlisted as a group to help find out who she is.

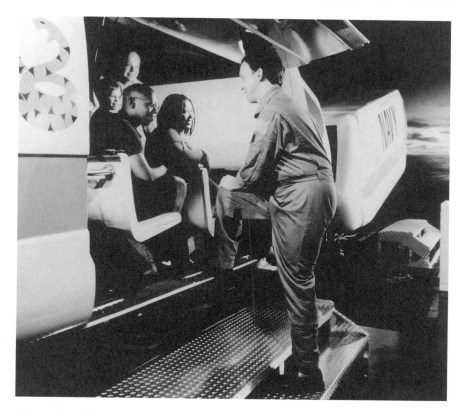

In *Navy: Technology at Sea*, the serious message of the nation's defense was combined with the excitement of two flight simulators using projection screens and hydraulic arms to create the physical sensations of a real military aircraft in flight.

A well-known local anchorman and actors were filmed to provide clues in a series of videoclips. Imaging technologies were programmed to help students toward a solution. One computer station magnified animal hair, for example, to test traces of fur on the mystery woman's coat. Childhood photos could be fed into face-aging computers to help establish identity.

The "Mystery Lab" succeeded almost from the day it was introduced in 1994. Early on, Museum staff members were intrigued with how the mystery was solved, how each group of students approached it a little differently. As the solution was pieced together, key breakthroughs did not always come from the usual stars of the class. Sometimes they came from the quiet ones, other times from the talkative class members who had trouble getting good grades. In this way, the "Mystery Lab" proved an important assumption of the Museum's education strategy—that different children have different kinds of intelligence, and learning laboratories should try to cater to them all.

LEARNING LABS BROADENED the reach of the Museum of Science and Industry among youngsters who might otherwise lack meaningful exposure to science and technology. The Museum's strong educational mission inspired other plans toward the same objective in the early 1990s. Among them was the Science Club Network, a project designed to get students in neighborhoods throughout the city interested in after-school science projects.

Established in 1992 with a $790,000 grant from the National Science Foundation, the Science Club Network was designed to reach out to youngsters and get them to devote a portion of their free time to learning about science and technology. Branch science clubs—mostly located at neighborhood drop-in centers—teach hands-on principles of construction, electricity and other subjects. The idea is for kids to work together and discover that pursuing these things is not just serious, but also fun.

Just how well it worked was evident at one of the early events for the entire network, the Science Club Jamboree in May 1995. Clubs from all over the city were invited to the Museum for demonstrations, seminars and other activities. The climax of the day came when each club was asked to plan and construct a model electric car and race it on a track. Most participants knew the basics from earlier lessons in engineering and motors. The challenge was for each group to design something quickly, assemble it and outperform the rest.

Adult supervision was minimal, and jamboree organizers were definitely worried when they saw a group from the Midtown Center, boys from a tough Northwest Side neighborhood, just sitting around. While the other clubs were building, the Midtown group looked baffled by the assignment.

As it turned out, they weren't baffled at all. They were just thinking. Eventually the boys came up with the most radical design of the competition—a strange-looking contraption with two wheels placed side by side. The Midtown group got some jeers when they built it. It didn't look like a car, some said. It was sure to tumble over. It didn't, of course, and to almost everyone's delight, it ran away with top honors. The experience was enjoyable, but it also transmitted indelible messages about technology. The most powerful one was that innovation sometimes risks embarrassment but is often very sweet indeed.

THE UNCOMMON CLASSROOM was taking many forms. Generally, it meant that youngsters, parents, and others were interacting with the Museum in new and more intensive ways. In a few cases, the Museum became an extension of the common classroom, as it did with the Bradwell School on Chicago's South Side.

This experiment began with Hulon Johnson, the principal of Bradwell who was long-frustrated by science education in virtually all inner city schools. Problems were well-known—Bradwell, like most other elementary schools in the Chicago school system, was woefully underequipped. Yet Johnson insisted that the city had resources, such as museums, that were clearly underused. So after discussions with the Museum's education department and administrators at the Board of Education, the principal devised a yearlong science program for all Bradwell students in the third through sixth grades.

Beginning in the fall of 1995, Bradwell students were bused to the Museum, where they spent their mornings. Students got some classroom work, but mostly they stayed in the exhibits learning about computers, biology, aeronautics, naval technology and other subjects. Johnson's objective was to excite children about science. "It is not a subject to be reserved for the privileged few," he said. Interestingly, Johnson designed his Museum program with adults in mind as well as the youngsters. While students were learning their lessons, Johnson believed, so were the teachers, who were also sadly lacking in science and technical skills.

WHILE THE MUSEUM SEARCHED for powerful ways to get the message across, the message was always a moving target. Science was changing, and some new lessons were increasingly urgent. Not long after he became president of the Museum, Dr. Kahn announced that one subject the Museum must soon address was the AIDS epidemic.

AIDS was obviously a pressing subject, and there was plenty of evidence that it was mishandled by many educational institutions. In some cases, the politics of the epidemic were too difficult for wide discussion in public schools. In other cases, museums that addressed the subject flooded visitors with so much detailed information that they quickly lost all but the most ambitious readers. As the disease spread and became a vital national concern, the Museum of Science and Industry's challenge was to overcome these obstacles with lessons about the disease that could reach every visitor, from adults all the way down to schoolchildren.

The subject was potentially explosive, but the objective of the AIDS exhibit was clear from the beginning—to explain how people and science can work together to control a deadly epidemic. The developers were also clear about what the exhibit was not. "This is not the 'Quilt Project,'" said one of them, referring to a late-'80s campaign to create an enormous quilt in commemoration of the tens of thousands of lives lost to AIDS. In this case, the goals of the exhibit were to increase the visitor's knowledge about the biology of HIV, AIDS and the immune system. It would specify the kinds of behavior that reduce risk. With a foundation of clear-eyed science, it would also foster humane attitudes toward persons affected by the disease.

AIDS: The War Within demonstrated that a serious subject could be
addressed with imagery vivid enough to interest visitors of all ages.
The exhibit itself was designed as an imaginary invasion site armed with
a sophisticated but fragile line of defense—the human immune system.

The difficulties in achieving these goals—with a complex disease and a
swirl of social issues—were well known to James Kahn and Barry Aprison. Earlier, the two had spearheaded an effort called the National AIDS Exhibit Con-
sortium, with eight museums sharing in the design and production of a series
of traveling exhibits. The problem, simply put, was to get ample information
across without using enormous text panels that no one would read, and to create interest in the subject without inflaming controversy that could easily overshadow any message.

The Museum's permanent AIDS exhibit, entitled *AIDS: The War Within*,
opened in 1995 after a planning process that lasted more than two years. This
became a groundbreaking event which drew interest from both the museum
community and the news media nationwide. Just as important for the Museum,

however, was what the process taught about addressing a difficult subject in an exhibit designed for people of all ages. A principal lesson was the importance of advice and counsel not just from scientists and designers, but from many people in the community as well. Among those involved by exhibit developers were AIDS social workers and people living with the virus and the disease; no one was better at articulating the many social issues connected with HIV and AIDS. Others that the Museum consulted in this process represented a group that needed this information the most—youngsters in the first stages of sexual activity.

Meetings with students were anything but encouraging at first. When members of the exhibit team interviewed seventh- and eighth-graders from schools near the Museum, they were shocked by some students' misconceptions. Strangely, many young people turned out to be unexpectedly sophisticated about the terminology of AIDS; they knew a range of acronyms like HIV (human immunodeficiency virus) and NIH (National Institutes of Health) as well as they knew the Chicago Bulls lineup. At the same time, they also believed in wildly inaccurate theories about the epidemic—one was that AIDS got started as part of a government research project gone wrong. Moreover, "safe sex" was just words to many of them. Many boys were completely unaware that they were responsible for prevention as much as girls were. By the end of the meetings, the team from the Museum was more convinced than ever that the exhibit they were working on could have high impact on the public and especially youth.

Other people brought into the process were from health and government organizations as well as charitable and activist groups. Many of these individuals composed an advisory committee that became indispensable in making the exhibit developers understand what worked in AIDS education, and how "hot-button" issues like homosexuality and drug use might be approached objectively. There was rarely total agreement among all the people. A Catholic organization, for example, dropped out because of the importance of condoms in the exhibit, though they continued to offer informal advice. A young AIDS activist became concerned when a section on sexual transmission was illustrated with a picture of a heterosexual couple. Consensus was sought if not always achieved. Ultimately, the exhibit was designed to reach the largest and most mainstream population possible.

As the message took form, so did the medium and the overall look of the exhibit. Responsibility for the design was awarded to Tom Owen, of St. Louis, after a nationwide search. Owen had long experience in stage and set design and naturally looked for theatrical images that might draw visitors into a subject that was anything but entertaining. Owen's first thought was soap operas, which he believed might evoke a sense of drama equal to the subject. He then arrived at the comic strip concept.

The idea of blown-up panels in comic-book style had accessibility yet seriousness. Simultaneously, Owen, Aprison and Marvin Pinkert imagined an elaborate invasion image. HIV cells magnified millions of times would permeate the walls and columns of the exhibit space. Large illustrations of heroic characters defending against the attack would accompany scientific information about AIDS prevention. With impact akin to that of pop artist Roy Lichtenstein's work, oversized and colorful panels would tell a story in an unthreatening but deadly serious way.

The genius of *AIDS: The War Within* was that it spoke to many people. Young and old alike could be drawn into the art. Other aspects of the exhibit worked on other levels—with videos and interactive computers to explain viruses, the immune system and other more delicate subjects such as sex and transmission. The exhibit remained dramatic but objective, a difficult balance which Museum staff members believed they achieved because they collaborated with many experts.

There was one interest group, however, that took the exhibit team by surprise. It was the Illinois Pro-Life Action League, activists who were angry—incongruously, Aprison thought—over the display of condoms. In the wake of some early publicity about the Museum's AIDS project, the prospective exhibit became the subject of the league's telephone hotline. For several days a recorded message ridiculed the Museum's "condom exhibit" and reaffirmed the belief that abstinence from sex outside marriage was the only solution to the AIDS epidemic.

Pro-life protests did not last long. The anti-Museum recording disappeared from the organization's hotline when other issues replaced it. A few protesters came to the exhibit's opening, but they disappeared when asked to leave. Ultimately the controversy revealed that a few members of the pro-life group, far from distrusting the Museum of Science and Industry, said they admired it and apparently decided to quit an issue little connected to abortion.

THE MUSEUM OF SCIENCE AND INDUSTRY has endured a series of controversies over the years, though they have rarely clouded its purpose. Early on, the founders battled financial woes caused by Chicago political figures. Later, the coming of Lenox Lohr brought the Museum up against a community of scholars who disapproved of the Major's de facto partnership with private industry. In the 1950s, the visit of Soviet Foreign Minister Molotov to the Museum unleashed marchers and pickets, as did a number of other exhibits that examined science and technology in Iron Curtain countries.

There have been other examples of turbulence, which may seem strange for a Museum that is best known for its relationship with children. Still, demonstrators with different political agendas have appeared at this Museum more often than most other cultural institutions in Chicago. Reasons may revolve around the nature of the relationship that the Museum of Science and Industry has forged with several generations of visitors.

What characterizes this relationship? Partly it is a deep emotional connection. Even before it opened, the institution garnered enormous public interest—so powerful was its mission to people from almost every segment of American society. Since then, the Museum has continued to strike a commanding and resonant chord in many exhibits, particularly through its great icons. For decades, visitors have returned again and again with children and now grandchildren to relive a part of their youth in the *U-505* or the *Fairy Castle*.

Most of all, the Museum of Science and Industry elicits a response that applies to children and adults in equal measure. That response is intense curiosity. No other Museum makes people wonder about such an array of phenomena, about sound waves, about the miracle of birth and the mechanics of orbiting satellites. At its best, the Museum has the power to open up that curiosity and fill it with lessons about science, technology and sometimes about humanity itself.

The Museum of Science and Industry possesses a deep-down knack for making people curious. Today, the quality that makes the *Coal Mine* such an enduring exhibit is hardly cutting-edge technology; rather it is a realistic and partly mysterious environment that continues to enchant. The same can be said for the *U-505*, the *Whispering Gallery* and many other exhibits.

The importance of visitors and the incisive curiosity that they bring was highlighted at another major event of recent years, a live television hookup between the space shuttle *Endeavour* and a group of students at the Henry Crown Space Center. It was an interview with Dr. Mae Jemison, the first African-American woman in space and a native Chicagoan. During the interview, Dr. Jemison discussed the experiments she was involved in during the flight. She told about biofeedback as a way to control the health of astronauts on the mission.

The most remarkable moment, however, came when a youngster eleven or twelve years old asked: "What did it feel like when you reached max Q?" Jemison smiled, obviously surprised at such a technical question, and explained, for those who did not know, that max Q is the point of maximum pressure during takeoff.

In fact, the question was more memorable than the answer. It indicated that one youngster, at least, was less impressed with the *Endeavour* or this remarkable feat of television engineering than with the idea that he might experience max Q someday himself. Once again, it rang out loud and clear that looking to the future is what the Museum of Science and Industry is all about.

Abbreviations

    CAP   Chicago Architectural Photographing Company

    MSI   Museum of Science and Industry

Pg. vi, photograph by C. D. Arnold/W. H. Jackson, MSI Archives; pg. ix, photograph by Bruce Powell, MSI Archives; pg. x, photograph by Bruce Powell, MSI Archives; pg. xiii, photograph by CAP, MSI Archives; pg. xiv, photograph by Bruce Powell, MSI Archives; pg. xviii, MSI Archives; pg. 5, photograph by CAP, MSI Archives; pg. 8, reprinted with permission from Texaco Inc.; pg. 12, MSI Archives; pg. 17, MSI Archives; pg. 29, reprinted with permission from *New York Times* Pictures; pg. 34, photograph by CAP, MSI Archives; pg. 41, photograph by CAP, MSI Archives; pg. 50, photograph by CAP, MSI Archives; pg. 53, photograph by CAP, MSI Archives; pg. 55, photograph by CAP, MSI Archives; pg. 57, photograph by CAP, MSI Archives; pg. 62, photograph by Roy Meller, MSI Archives; pg. 72, photograph by CAP, MSI Archives; pg. 77, permission granted by Westinghouse Electrical Corporation, MSI Archives; pg. 85, (top) courtesy of the Connecticut Valley Historical Museum, Springfield, MA., (bottom) *Sun Times* Photo Files; pg. 87, MSI Archives; pg. 89, MSI Archives; pg. 91, photograph by Vories Fisher, MSI Archives; pg. 93, reprinted with permission from BF Goodrich, MSI Archives; pg. 97, MSI Archives; pg. 101, MSI Archives; pg. 105, MSI Archives; pg. 115, Photo Ideas, Inc. (no. 4-970); pg. 119, *Sun Times* Photo Files; pg. 120, MSI Archives; pg. 123, MSI Archives; pg. 129, MSI Archives; pg. 131, MSI Archives; pg. 133, Photo Ideas, Inc. (no. 11-740); pg. 135, MSI Archives; pg. 138, MSI Marketing Dept.; pg. 140, MSI Archives; pg. 148, Photo Ideas, Inc. (no. 5-289); pg. 151, MSI Archives; pg. 156, photograph by Art Wise; pg. 159, MSI Marketing Dept.; pg. 164, photograph by Don Jiskra; pg. 169, photograph by Charles Eshelman, Chicago, IL.; pg. 171, photograph by Loren Santow; pg. 174, photograph by Charles Eshelman, Chicago, IL.

THIS BOOK WAS CONCEIVED in a meeting with Dr. James S. Kahn, the visionary president of the Museum of Science and Industry. Dr. Kahn believed that a comprehensive narrative of the Museum's history might demonstrate the relationship between the early ideals of the institution and the ambitious plans of the 1990s and beyond.

To achieve this goal, many, many sources of information were indispensable. Among them was the Museum's rich archive, which consists of letters, reports, scrapbooks, ephemera and volumes of other material saved by a succession of historically-minded people at the Museum.

Several people were entrusted with the archive, located in the Collections Department of the Museum, in the period during which this book was researched and written. Laura Graedel, current archivist, provided constant enthusiasm and expert assistance. Keith Gill and Sue Eleuterio also assisted with these records, which represent the heritage not just of one institution but of the city of Chicago at large. Also in the Collections Department, Michael Sarna, Tim Wauters, Juergen Droggemueller, and Karen Lukasik were helpful in opening marvelous doors to the past.

A previous book on the Museum, *A Continuing Wonder* by Herman Kogan, published in 1973, was also indispensable in researching this one. Beside providing a rich narrative, Kogan's instinct for the grand themes of Chicago history provides a standard by which other local histories are measured.

Naturally, books of recent history depend upon reminiscences, oral histories and recollections of people personally involved in the episodes of the past. Among those generous with insight and perspective were two former presidents of the Museum, Daniel MacMaster and Victor Danilov, along with their wives, Sylvia MacMaster and Toni Dewey Danilov.

Other past employees interviewed included Bruce Mitchell, Bernice Martin, Lucy Nielsen, David Ucko, Mike Kwiatkowski, Otto Harringer, Kathleen Carpenter, Ted Swigon, Ted Ansbacher, Val Kass and Kirsten Ellenbogen. These people provided the narrative with a level of detail that otherwise would be missing.

Many current employees of the Museum gave generous amounts of time to this project. First among them was Carl Friedenberg, senior member of the Museum staff, whose memories are clear and extensive. Others included Marvin Pinkert, Steve Bishop, Barry Aprison, Jan Coffey, Pam Nelson, Mike Boersma, Matt Rothan, Mike Jehlik, Mike Levine, Frank Cycenas, Jill Finney, Jason Harris, Viki Diana, Diane McCain, Joe Shacter and Elizabeth Jackson.

Several trustees of the Museum provided invaluable observations about their work with the Museum. These included William Weiss, David Grainger and Cindy Pritzker.

Also helpful were people whose association with the Museum came through other means. Herman Sereika was an employee of Commonwealth Edison when he served as a popular master of ceremonies at the company's exhibit in the '40s, *Electric Theater*. Ernie Zichal was manager of public relations for Illinois Bell and was a central figure in a succession of telephone exhibits. Glen Fleck and Bruce Burdick, now designers in California, worked with the late Charles Eames in the early '60s on IBM's ground-breaking exhibit, *Mathematica . . . The World of Numbers and Beyond*. R. P. Berglund of IBM Corp. was also helpful with insights into *Mathematica*. Dr. Helen Button was donor of the famous embryo collection and was generous in telling that story.

Richard Kreusser is the son of the Museum's second executive director, Otto Kreusser, and provided fascinating details of his late father's career, and especially the design and opening of the Museum's famous *Coal Mine*. David Barrow, a model railroad enthusiast in Austin, Texas, was a source of information about Minton Cronkhite, the original designer of *The Museum & Santa Fe Railroad*, as was Andy Sperandeo, editor of *Model Railroader Magazine*.

Jerre Levy, a biopsychologist at the University of Chicago, worked on the exhibit *My Daughter, the Scientist*, created in the '80s, and reconstructed some of the important themes of that exhibit. Robert Beck, scientific imaging expert at the University of Chicago, discussed his early role in the exhibit *IMAGING: The Tools of Science*.

The Museum's relationship with Argonne National Laboratory was described to the author by a number of people, including John Farmakes, who managed early exhibits for Argonne, and Jack Holl, historian of the lab. Some important information about Chicago's public television station, WTTW, came from Joel Sternberg, a professor at St. Xavier College and a historian of the station. George Howard provided additional information about WTTW in its earliest years when it was located at the Museum.

Devereux Bowly, a longtime Hyde Park resident, provided many interesting insights into the development of the Museum. Bowly is working on a book about Julius Rosenwald and was helpful in the research of this one. He has maintained an interest in the Museum from a young age, especially its architecture. Susan Crown, descendant of Henry Crown, was kind enough to reconstruct the events that led to the conception and funding of the Henry Crown Space Center.

Archives at other institutions played a part in this book, including the University of Illinois at Chicago, where Special Collections librarian Mary Ann Bamberger was most helpful; and the Chicago Park District, where Julia Sniderman and Bart Ryckbosch helped sort through archives about the long-time relationship between Chicago's parks and one of its famous museums.

Perhaps most importantly, thanks go to people who have lived with this book and attended to many details over a long period of time. Nancy Dove, the Museum's director of marketing, and Marianne Beaudoin, manager of the creative group, deserve credit for keeping this book project alive.

Kim Coventry, with whom the author has enjoyed a long relationship, served as the producer for this book, shepherding the project through many, sometimes arduous, steps. Barbara Anderson was an editor of sensitivity. Joan Sommers provided predictably skilled design.

Among the many people involved, one person stands out as a most reliable and generous participant. Eileen Cabrera, assistant to the president, maintained enthusiasm, understanding and patience for this project over a period that might have exhausted someone less generous. She has the author's sincere gratitude.

Without the assistance of these and others, this book could not have been completed. To them all go the author's, and I hope the readers', thanks.

Jay Pridmore

LP MCD
McDermid, Val.
The grave tattoo.

DATE	ISSUED TO